'The Goode Mr Garbet of Wem'

The Life of the Revd. Samuel Garbet, M.A. of Wem, Shropshire 1685–1756

Beryl M. Jones

bridge
books

Wrexham

First published in Wales in 2001
by
Bridge Books
61 Park Avenue
Wrexham
LL12 7AW

© 2001 Beryl M. Jones

All Rights Reserved.
No part of this publication may be reproduced,
stored in a retrieval system, or transmitted
in any form or by any means, electronic,
mechanical, photocopying, recording or
otherwise, without the prior permission
of the Copyright holder.

ISBN 1-872424-74-0

A CIP catalogue entry for this book
is available from the British Library

Printed and bound by
MFP, Stretford, Manchester

Contents

Acknowledgements	v
Preface	vii
The Goode Mr Garbet of Wem	11
Education	17
The Ministry	20
Marriage and Wem Society	25
The Garbets settle in Wem	32
The Schoolmaster	43
The Local Historian	51
Conclusion	60
Appendices	
I The Church Lewn for Wem	64
II Register of pupils of Wem Grammar School, 1719–37	69
Notes	74

Illustrations and Maps

Area of Shropshire associated with Samuel Garbet	ix
Area around Wem associated with Samuel Garbet	x
Norton Farm, Wroxeter	12
Table of Descent of Samuel Garbet of Wem	14
The Groves, Walcot	15
St Andrews Church, Wroxeter	18
Newtown Chapel	21
Great Ness Church	21
Headmaster's House, Wem	23
Edstaston Church	25
White Horse, Wem	31
St Peter & St Paul's Parish Church, Wem	33
Samuel Garbet's Notebook	35
Class List of Wem Grammar School	45
Letter from a parent, 1716	47
Samuel Garbet's map of Wem (section)	55
Samuel Garbet's map of Wem (section)	56
Samuel Garbet's grave	62

Preface

This study examines the life and times of the Reverend Samuel Garbet, one of the earliest local historians of Shropshire. Although he was born in the parish of Wroxeter, he spent most of his working life in the town of Wem and is buried in the churchyard of Edstaston Chapel near that town. His memorial is, without doubt, his *The History of Wem*, which he wrote during his later days. Unlike his near neighbour and contemporary, Richard Gough, author of *The History of Myddle*, of whom a great deal is known, very little has appeared in print about Samuel Garbet. There is a short paragraph in the *Dictionary of National Biography*, mainly derived from the few clues gleaned from *The History of Wem*.

However, some years ago, over six hundred documents were discovered in Wrexham which included a wide variety of Garbet papers including letters, diaries, accounts, wills and inventories.[1] His book, *The History of Wem* is noted as a secondary source in many bibliographies of the local landscape and county histories of Shropshire. This new material should,therefore, be used as a tribute to this learned gentleman, who contributed so much to the recording of the history of Shropshire, the county of his birth and working life.

It has been a privilege for me, as a local historian, to be allowed to examine, catalogue and index this previously unknown collection of important personal papers belonging to Samuel Garbet. It has given me the opportunity to uncover the private and professional activities of a rural cleric, who rightly deserves recognition as an early local historian. He is probably unknown outside the county of his birth, Shropshire, where he is remembered for writing one of the earliest historical accounts —*The History of Wem* which, although compiled during the early 18th century, was not published until 1818, some sixty years after Garbet's death.

The essence of this study, is to seek and reveal the unwitting evidence from this important collection and to portray the character of this learned gentleman. The analysis of his personal papers, his income, accounts, inventories and letters will reveal his life style and the importance placed on his social role in the local society of his day. This man of many talents who, as an ordained curate, licensed schoolmaster, translator and cartographer, added so much to the study of local history within the county of Shropshire.

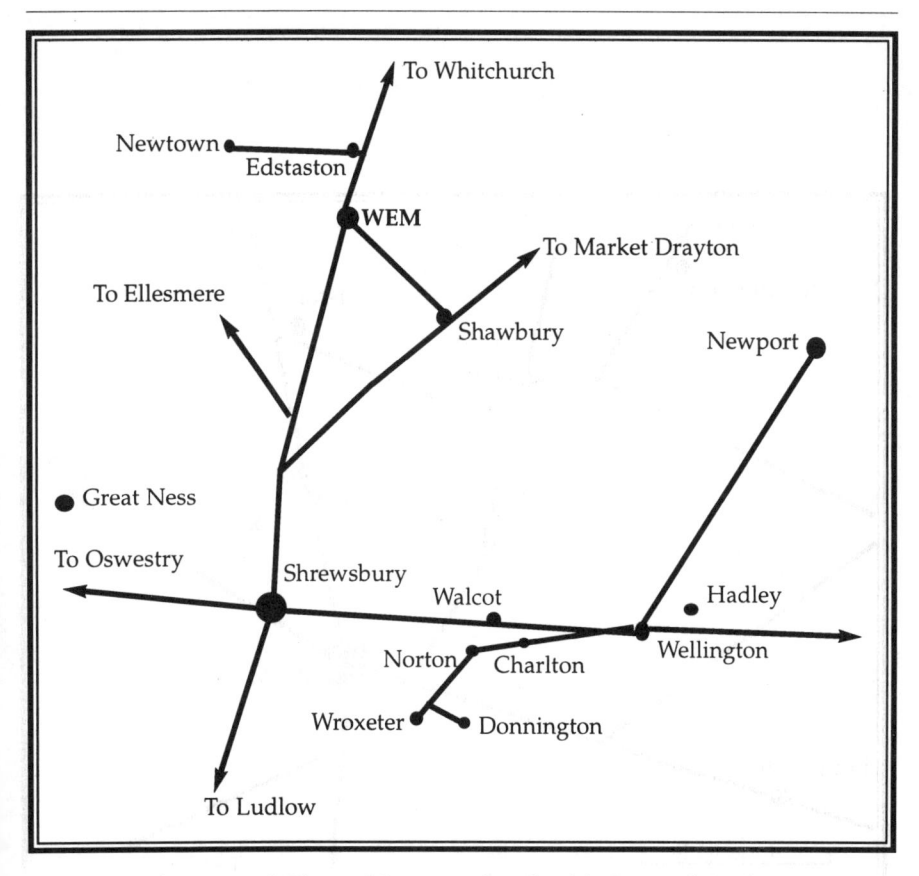

The area of Shropshire associated with Samuel Garbet

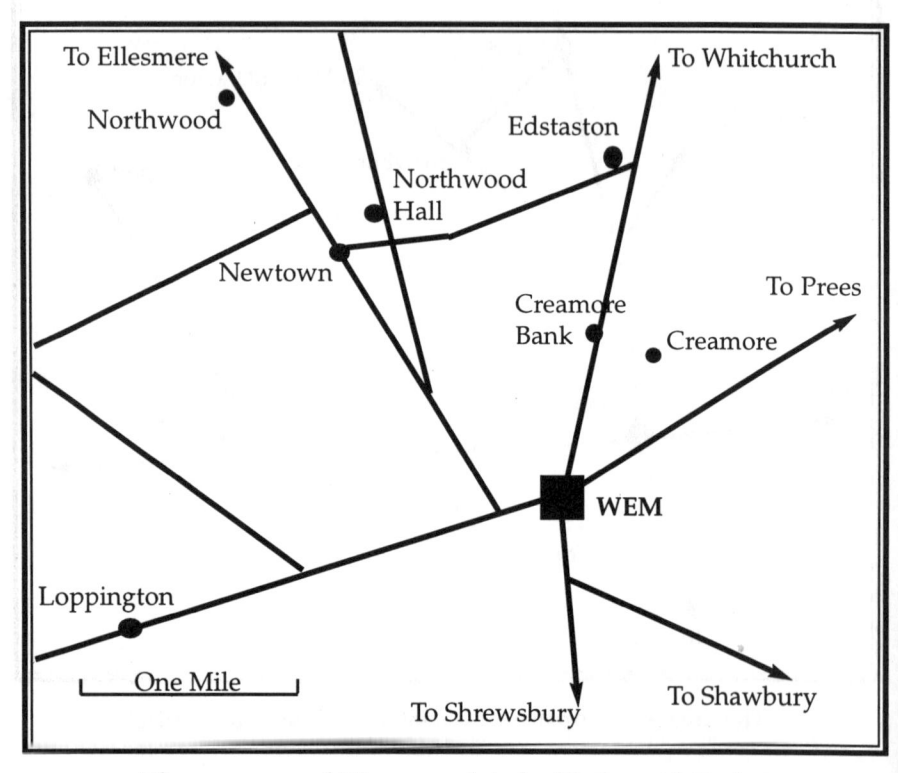

The area around Wem associated with Samuel Garbet

'The Goode Mr Garbet of Wem'

1706 Sept 22nd, I was ordained Deacon at Eccleshall [Staffordshire] by good Dr. Hough, Bishop of Lichfield and Coventry. I had my Testimonial from Christchurch College, my Title from Mr Binnel, Vicar of Leighton and Rector of Sheinton.
Not long after at his request, I preached at Leighton in ye morning & crossing the Severn in a boat, at Sheinton in the evening.
But my first essay was made at Newtown Chapel, in ye parish of Wem, my father bore me company, and we lodged two nights with John Dean, who kept ye White Horse. Little did I then think that I should pass the the greatest part of my life in this town.[2]

This visit to Wem by Samuel Garbet, was made some six years before he made a permanent move to the town, initially as second master at the Wem Free Grammar School, then soon after as curate of Edstaston Chapel in the parish. Today, he is remembered in the town not only as a reverend gentleman and a noted schoolmaster, but also as one of the earliest local historians in Shropshire, although his *History of Wem* was not published until sixty years after his death.

Samuel was born on 18 January 1685/6 and baptised five days later. He was the son of Francis and Anne Garbet, his mother being one of the many daughters of James Cleaton of The Banks, Oakengates near Wellington (now part of Telford). He was born at the home of his grandfather and namesake, Samuel Garbet, on the Norton estate in the parish of Wroxeter, but by the end of the year his parents had moved to the Walcot estate in the parish of Wellington.

Samuel was the eldest of three children, his sister Elizabeth, born 15 July 1688, married Thomas Studley, who, as Samuel wrote, 'Stole her away',[3] and had by him, a son Francis.*

---

* *On graduation from Cambridge, Francis became successively curate of Rodington, Stottesdon and Wenlock where he died on 17 April 1747. He was a troublesome thorn in Samuel Garbet's side through the many family disputes over inheritances, in particular when Samuel discovered that he (Francis) had cut off the entail of the Wellington estate, which had been bought with Samuel's money. Samuel wrote that he had never 'committed a greater oversight than leaving it in his power to do me this injurey. As when the final settlement of the Walcot estate was drawn up, I did not understand*

Norton Farm, Wroxeter, Samuel Garbet's birthplace.

Samuel's younger brother James (born in 1693 at Walcot) served an apprenticeship with a Mr Jenks, an apothecary of the Wyle Cop, Shrewsbury, and became in his own right, an eminent apothecary in the same town and, to quote Samuel, 'Built two very genteel houses in the High Street'.[4]

The Garbets
The Garbets are best described as having been land-owning petty gentry, many of whom appear in the records as gentlemen. Samuel reckoned that the founder of the family was 'one Robert Garbet, because he was the first to be raised to the degree of Gentleman'. Robert Garbet was one of the original Yeomen of the Guard to King Henry VII and from the device borne on his arms, Samuel believed that he was an Ensign or Standard Bearer. He also believed that Robert was much favoured by the King who rewarded his services, not only with an 'Escutcheon',[5] but also with a considerable estate, namely Acton Burnell in Shropshire which, in 1485, was forfeited to the

> this point in law, and my attorney was not so good as to explain it to me'. He went on to say that 1747 was his great 'climacterical' year, it had liked to have proved fatal to him, and ended with the interesting note that, on Sunday the 29 March, as he was reading morning prayers in Edstaston Chapel, he perceived a a sudden eruption of the piles, I crushed up the tumors which afterwards inflamed by the Apothecaries wrong application.

Crown by Francis the Lord Lovel, for his adherence to Richard III.

The family enjoyed the Acton Burnell estates for no more than three generations before it divided with one branch settling on the Middleton estate in the parish of Bitterly near Ludlow and the elder branch moving first to Condover and later to Buttingham. This branch remained Roman Catholic, but nevertheless kept in constant and regular touch with their protestant Middleton cousins.

Samuel's great grandfather was Francis Garbet (born 1575), who was educated at Balliol College, Oxford and, being pleased with college life and 'Having sufficient provision',[6] resigned his inheritance of the Middleton estate to his brothers. In 1609, he was prevailed upon to accept the vicarage of Wroxeter, where he remained throughout the Civil War. He taught logic to Richard Baxter the 'Puritan Divine' who published many books, and always gave Mr Garbet the character of a faithful, learned and peaceable divine. To show his gratitude for the many favours received from Francis Garbet, Baxter sent him a bound copy of each of his books as a present. Francis married twice, on both occasions to very wealthy women, which enabled him to leave a considerable fortune to his son Samuel of Norton. The will of Francis Garbet written in 1658 and proved in 1661 mentions a daughter Mary Baxter, and the children 'of my sonne Baxter'.*

Samuel Garbet of Norton, the grandfather of Samuel of Wem, was born in the rambling vicarage of Wroxeter in 1624 and continued to live there after his marriage and the birth of his eldest son Francis (27 January 1657) and his second son Charles (1659). On the death of his father in 1661, Samuel and his family were obliged to quit the vicarage. With his considerable fortune, Samuel Garbet of Norton, being a gentleman farmer, moved from Wroxeter and settled in the Hall at Preston Brocklehurst, the principal estate of Samuel Wingfield, Esq. Whilst Samuel was at Preston, Mr Wingfield offered to sell him all his estate in that parish of which a greater part was then in lease for lives, upon a small reserved rent. Samuel Garbet, however, declined the the offer as he was unwilling to run so far into debt. However, not long after, he had reason to regret his caution for, within a few years, the leases dropped and then the estate was worth double the price for which he might have bought it. By 1680, following the death of his second son (also named

---

* *Francis Garbet died in 1661 but, without a full inventory, it is difficult to assess his personal wealth. His will instructs his executors to pay just £4 to the poor of the parish. The few appraisals are to the 'books' in his study — assessed at £60; a horse and saddle at £4, and wearing apparel at £10. His daughters, Mary Baxter and Beatrice Farmer, were to receive sets of books and all his grand children just two lambs apiece. The remainder of his property, including all his debts, he left to his eldest son Samuel an inheritance which enabled him to enjoy a most comfortable life style.*

Robert Garbett
of Acton Burnell

Mrs Scriven = Thomas = Margery Wood
of Cundover of of Burton

Thomas
of Cundover

Roger
of Middleton

Mary Detton = Francis = Joyce Hatten
Vicar of Wroxeter

Thomas
drowned in the Severn

Samuel
of Norton

= Christian Bennet

Anne Cleaton = Francis
of Walcot

Samuel
of Emanuel College
Cambridge

Samuel
of Wem
Clerk

= Anna Edwards
of Great Ness

Samuel
of Wem
Clerk

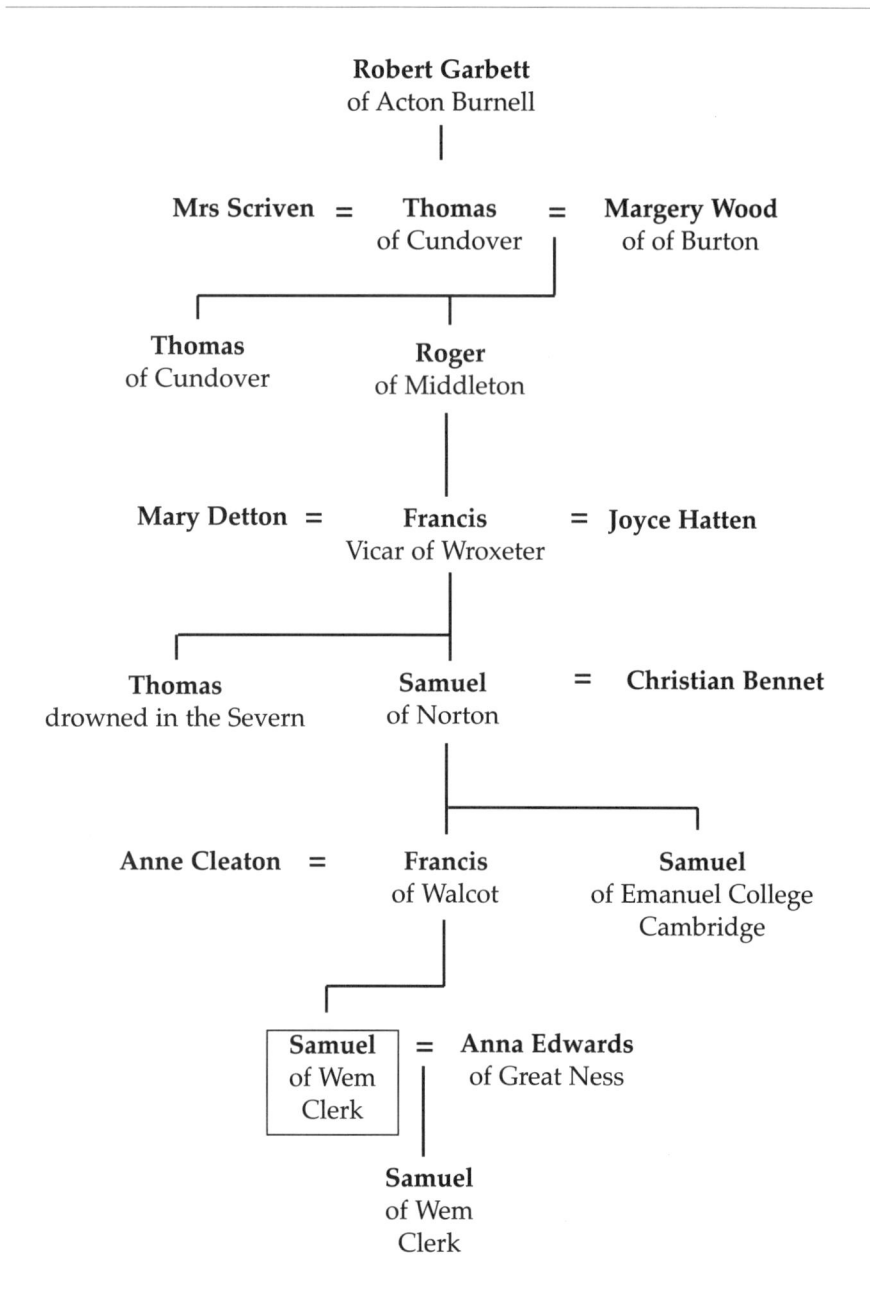

Table of Descent of Samuel Garbet of Wem

The Groves, Walcot, Samuel Garbet's childhood home. The house is now called The Grange.
[Courtesy of Mr Prinold]

Samuel) he was living on the Cronkhill estate near Attingham Park, Atcham. At this time he bought from Edward Kynaston, Esq. of Albrightlea, two messuages of land, with the whole of the Walcot estate in the parish of Wellington for only £730 and, as Samuel of Wem wrote in his later years, 'That the value of lands is advanced almost double since that time. He never laid out money to greater advantage — his estate remains to be enjoyed by his posterity'.[7] The Walcot estate had been bought for the intended marriage of his eldest son Francis to Ann Cleaton and on the 16 January 1684 he settled it on Francis and his heirs in exchange for £200 paid him by Francis, which was the marriage portion paid by James Cleaton, Gentleman, of The Banks, Oakengates.

Having secured his son's (Francis) future at the Walcot estate, Samuel was now settled at Norton in the parish of Wroxeter, which he leased from Edward Kynaston, Albrightlea. Samuel of Wem described Norton as the best farm in the town, with a good house and dove house, which was on lease for life along with a lesser farm for a term of years.

Samuel Garbet of Norton, who died in 1708, aged 84, is buried at Wroxeter. His grandson Samuel wrote of him: 'He was tall of stature and of sanguine complexion. His education under so strict a father influenced his whole life and conversation. He constantly went to church, and daily read the scriptures to his family, improving them by his example, as well as the instruction he gave them. He was very temperate and regular, quiet and peaceable, had good natural parts and a competent share of learning'.[8] Of his grandmother, Christian Bennett, he wrote 'She was a little woman, but one of the best, I ever knew, she was so meek as to never to fall into a passion; so prudent, as always to endeavour to pacify those that did. In short I do not remember her speak an unhandsome word or do an ill thing'.[9]

In 1694, Francis Garbet of Walcot was elected as one of the High Constables of the Hundred of Bradford South, a position of considerable local importance. Though service was compulsory, there was no legal provision for any reimbursement for carrying out the duty, and the time allotted for this appointment varied from hundred to hundred. In some it was for just one year, in others for three years and in the remainder until the appointee chose to retire. However, a study by the Webb's[10] shows that in more than half the courts, the office became one for life. Persons serving in this position were usually from the humbler gentry, small freeholders or yeomen. In 1697, Francis Garbet was taking the tithes for the township of Walcot at a rent of £8 *per annum* and held them whilst he continued to reside there. This information is recorded in Francis's notebook [SGP Notebook 6] along with cures for animals, particularly horses, with herbs being the main ingredient. There he lists every male in the township of Walcot in the Parish of Wellington and their assessments. Francis Garbet, the Groves Farm, Walcot (now called the Grange) always received the highest assessment for land tax, repairs of bridges, the military, the carrying away of vagabonds and, in 1705, the building of a new gaol and the house of correction and for maimed soldiers. Charges for county and townships are listed covering the period 1694 until his death in 1737. About 1730, Francis and his wife Ann left Walcot to live with their son James in the High Street, Shrewsbury and the Walcot estate was leased to William Hazlehurst.

Ann Garbet died on 22 October 1736 aged 77, and her son Samuel wrote of her:

> Whilst she was at Walcot, she kept a good house and practised hospitality and managed her country business with equal care and industry. She would not be idle herself. or suffer any about her to be so, warm she was in her resentments but shew'd much good nature to those that pleased her. Being averse to disimulation, she used to speak her mind with great freedom. The ill state of her beloved son James, gave her much concern, that it broke her constitution and shortened her days.[11]

She was not long survived by her husband, who died on the 30 January 1737 aged 80.

According to Samuel, Francis Garbet 'Was low of stature, he had been strong and active and his ruddy countenance continued even in old age. When he was young he delighted in a good horse, and was then very subject to the headache, which he relieved by cutting off his hair. He was sober and never known to be disordered with drink, he was careful, industrious, patient, good natured, pious and devout. Subject to some starts of passion, but they were soon over'.[12]

Francis and Anne Garbet lie buried with their son James in a vault in St Alkmund's church, Shrewsbury.

It would appear that the Garbet family enjoyed a comfortable position amongst the petty gentry of Shropshire. They were freeholders with a considerable estate or, as Samuel wrote, 'gentlemen farmers'.[13]

Education
Samuel Garbet entered Christchurch College, Oxford on 12 June 1700, at the tender age of fourteen and a half years, prior to this he had, over the previous ten years, attended no fewer than five schools.

His first petty school, in which he started aged four, was at Charlton and from there he moved in 1692 to Oakengates, boarding with his grandfather Cleaton at The Banks. In 1694, he was attending school in Wellington and there had the privilege of dining with his father, on the occasions that Francis Garbet, as High Constable of Bradford Hundred, attended the court meeting there. In 1695/6 he was sent to a Mr Roe, who taught at Hadley after leaving Wem Free Grammar School. Robert Roe was a gentleman, born at Arleston near Wellington where his father had been a noted schoolmaster. In 1677, during his time as chief master at Wem School, the great fire of Wem took place. This devastated most of the town, destroying his dwelling house, (the birth place of Thomas Adams, the founder of the school) and reduced Roe to the necessity of living in the upper story of the school building. Samuel described Roe as 'A man of large stature, but of mean capacity so that he did neither shine in conversation nor was able to keep up the reputation of the school'.[14] Roe returned to Arleston, and not long afterwards purchased the Lordship of Hadley, where he taught private school in the manor house. It was here that Samuel records that he was taught 'The accidence of Grammar'.[15] Whilst there Samuel again boarded with grandfather Cleaton, receiving his board, 'Gratis',[16] at The Banks, for the Cleaton's house was just one mile from Hadley Manor. It was also at Hadley that Samuel sustained an injury, that must have made some impact for he vividly recalled the incident some fifty years later. He was apparently

St. Andrew's Church, Wroxeter, where Samuel Garbet's great-grandfather was vicar.

standing at the side of an archery butt, and was accidentally shot in the side of the nose by an arrow as he turned to look in the direction from whence it came.[17]

In 1696, Francis Garbet was informed by Richard, Lord Newport, that Samuel would be able to attend Donnington School free of charge, having been born in the parish of Wroxeter. Here Samuel was put under the care of Mr Markham, and was in the same class as Henry (afterwards the Earl of Bradford), Richard (the son of Justice Powell of Worthin) and Richard (son of Sir Edward Leighton of Wattlesbury). Donnington school had been founded in 1627 by Thomas Alcock, a yeoman of Wroxeter; who provided an endowment of twenty marks from lands in Edgerley. Thomas Alcock stipulated that the 'Master' should be appointed by the Newport family who were the Lords of the Manor of Wroxeter; and that free education should be given to the children of the parishes of Wroxeter and Uppington.

Before the outbreak of the Civil War, the school was held in Wroxeter village, possibly in the church: Richard Baxter 'The Puritan Divine' wrote of his schooldays there during 1627–31. The first Master was John Owen, who lived with Sir Richard Newport at Eyton on Severn, and taught Latin and Greek. Within twenty years of opening, the school moved to Donnington House, Donnington, and by 1674 the master was also perpetual curate of Uppington. This provision endured until 1879, the added income no doubt encouraging the master to remain at the school.

During Samuel's first year at Donnington, he lodged with grandfather Garbet at Norton, the house being less than a mile from the school. After the death of his grandmother, Christian Garbet, in 1698, Samuel was thought able to walk from his home at Walcot, although it was double the distance. 'Often did I trudge it afoot, but generally was favoured with a good horse'.[18] During one Whitsuntide holiday, both Samuel and his brother succumbed to the smallpox which left James with a badly pitted face but Samuel was fortunate to escape with no marks at all.

In 1700, Peter Edwards, a cousin who was later to become the headmaster at Wem Free Grammar School, prevailed upon Samuel's parents to allow him to go to Oxford one year earlier than they had intended. He arrived at Oxford on 8 June 1700, and four days later was entered at Christchurch College and matriculated at the University. He was admitted by Dr Hammond, the Sub Dean at Christchurch, at the request of Mr Markham (Samuel's master at Donnington school) who was related to Dr Hammond, and often stayed at his lodgings. Samuel records that:

> Mr William Adams,* a Shropshire man, editor of *Cornelius Nepos* was pitched upon as my tutor. I was once or twice at a lecture with him; but he did not give himself the trouble of reading any more tho' he had several gentlemen commoners for his pupils'.[19]

Samuel shared the same lodgings as his tutor, who often came in late from the tavern, and sat near his bed to converse freely. He impressed Samuel, who thought he was a great genius who wrote well in both prose and verse. According to archive sources at Christchurch College, Samuel matriculated

---

* *After the death of William Adams, a volume of his sermons was published by his executor, Dr Sacheverall [SGP/Y13].*

on 12 June 1700 as a servitor — an undergraduate who performed menial, but not onerous duties in return for his tuition. College records for this period are rather thin, especially with regard to the lower ranks of college members. However, it is known that in 1703 Samuel would have read Gracian's *Art of Prudence*, Bacon's *Essays*, Collier's *Essays* and some Homer, either the *Illiad* or the *Odyssey Book I*.[20]

In 1702, Samuel's diary records the visit to Oxford on August 26 of Queen Anne and Prince George of Denmark, whose guards rode around the coach, with drawn swords, and that the Queen was received at the lodgings of Dr Aldrich, Dean of Christchuch, who later became Rector of Wem. After supper, as the Queen went through a passage to her bed chamber, Samuel, together with other scholars knelt down, as she gave them her hand to kiss. The next morning he was caught by the Vice Chancellor, pressing for a full view of the Queen's departure, and was threatened with being sent 'To the Castle', and almost missed the noble entertainment provided for the Queen in the theatre.

During the summer of 1702 Samuel records that he 'went to the country for the first time'.[21] In 1703, the only item mentioned is that on 26 November 'I was in college during the most terrible storm of wind that was ever known in England'.[22] He took the degree of Batchelor of Arts on 23 May 1704 and had access to the university and college libraries, and dined every day at 'cookes shop'.[23] Part of 1705 was spent at Christchurch; but most of the year was spent at Walcot.

The Ministry
Samuel was ordained a deacon at Eccleshall on 22 September 1706. His testimonial came from Christchurch College, with his title from Mr Binnel, Vicar of Leighton and Rector of Sheinton who had invited Samuel to preach from the pulpit for the first time ever, at Leighton and Sheinton. Samuel's very first essay was presented at Newtown chapel in the parish of Wem on 27 October 1706.[24] On 9 February 1707 Samuel entered on the curacy of Great Ness, (alias Ness Strange), being recommended to the vicar, Mr Williams, 'By my very good friend Mr Lawrence, Vicar of Wrockwardine.'[25] This was some two and a half years after his graduation from Christchurch.

> I now laboured under some difficulties, being provided with few sermons, few books and of them, scarce any that were valuable. However, having the advantage of succeeding an old man, and an ordinary preacher. I had the happiness to please the people, and not the least reason to be dissatisfied with any of them; my salary was £20–0s–0d per year, besides the 'Surplice

The Goode Mr Garbet of Wem 21

Newtown 'Chapel'.

Great Ness Church.

Fees', which amounted to more or less, according as funeral sermons and mortuaries happened.[26] Mr Williams [vicar of Great Ness] intended that I should board with Mr Robert Edwards* at Great Ness, but not liking his table, I was, by one of the Langleys of Burcot, recommended to Mrs Wingfield of Alderton.[27]

In the summer of 1709 Samuel Garbet journeyed to Oxford where he took his Master's degree and was created Regent Master, and admitted to sit in convocation. On 29 June he preached at St Thomas's, Oxford and on 13 July at Ashington.

From February 1707 until May 1709, Samuel lodged with Mrs Martha Wingfield at Alderton Hall at the cost of £10 per annum. He now lived very happily, in a very 'regular' house where a plentiful table was kept, and where he had the convenience of a good horse, and here his diaries reveal a rare personal comment:

> My happiness was too great to be lasting, the son and some relations of Mrs. Wingfield, conceiving that she had too tender a kindness for me, resolved to separate us. So on 31st May 1709 I removed to the house of Mr Robert Edwards of Great Ness; 'and tho' my income was but small, I spared money to buy a watch, some Cane Chairs and a Table'.[28]

Martha Wingfield, the mother of six children, was the widow of Jonathan Wingfield, whose father had bought the Alderton Hall estate in 1640. When Samuel arrived there, Martha had been a widow for five years. The tithing book of Great Ness, a remarkable record of the great and small tithes paid by the parishoners, bears witness to the size of Martha Wingfield's estate, and another letter in the collection reveals that it was a known fact that Samuel and Martha were openly courting as Samuel was invited to attend a play in Wem 'and to be sure to bring Mrs Wingfield'.

On 23 February 1709, Samuel preached at the funeral service of Mr John Edwards (senior) of Great Ness, the father of his future wife. He records that 'A great number of gentlemen were present, the church could not contain the company'.[29]

On 17 August the same year, Mr Williams, the vicar of Great Ness died, and it is recorded that, all the parishioners joined in a petition to the Lord Chancellor that Samuel Garbet, curate might succeed him. This petition

---

* *Robert Edwards was later to become Samuel's brother-in-law, being the brother of Anna Edwards, who married Samuel in 1714.*

†*There are constant references in Samuel's diaries to the quality of the cooking at the Edward's family table, which was certainly not to his liking.*

The Headmaster's House, Adam's Free Grammar School, Wem.

failed, but Samuel continued to serve as curate, now to a Mr Collier who had previously served as curate at Edstaston Chapel in Wem parish and who was 'Second Master' at Wem school.* Collier succeeded Mr Williams in the vicarage at Great Ness in 1710 and two years later resigned from his post at Wem school, which he had so much neglected, that the trustees tried to have him removed. He was always very busy during the election of the knights of the shire, and it was on this score, that he was in good favour with Henry, Lord Newport, by whose interest he procured the appointment to Great Ness. Garbet describes Collier as being 'Of middle stature, with a sanguine complexion, his face being a little inflamed from the drink. He was not a scholar or a divine, but was well respected as a sportsman and a good companion'.[30]

Still determined to procure a vicarage, Samuel received a letter of recommendation from John Kynaston, Esq, of Hordley, to Mr Bromely, with another from Mrs Edwards of Ness (his future mother-in-law) to Mr Bromely's steward. He then took a long journey to Horseheath,

---

*John Collier was born in Gnosall parish in Staffordshire, and was educated at Newport school, Shropshire, and at Sydney College, Cambridge. As curate of Edstaston Chapel he was able to purchase a good house with a large garden which was in an alley between Noble Street and High Street in Wem.

Cambridgeshire, in an effort to obtain the rectory of Shrawardine in the parish adjoining to Great Ness.

> I supped with Mr Bromely, who next morning set out early to prosecute his election for the county of Cambridgeshire. On my return through Cambridge I was shewn King's College, but having no acquaintance in the university, I made but a short stay there.[31]
>
> The living I was in pursuit of, was given to one, whose chief merit was the soliciting of votes for his patron. He brought his wife, children and effects in a wagon, which he drove all the way himself, being much fitter for a wagonner than a Parson![32]

This quotation highlights Samuel's caustic sense of humour —or was it disappointment— as he had applied for no less than eight vicarages and had been rejected for every one.

On 11 March 1712, Samuel was unanimously elected second master of Wem Free Grammar School, but he did not begin to teach until after Lady Day. He, together with a Mr Edwards, Mr Gardener, Mr Cooke and Mr Watkins, boarded with a Mrs Williams who may have been the newly widowed wife of Mr Francis Williams, Chief Master of Wem School (who died in 1710, leaving a widow, one son and many daughters). Shortly after his arrival at the school, Samuel wrote:

> My school was near empty but I had the satisfaction to find it full very soon. Town and country concurred in giving both the Masters a good character, which established our reputations for eight to nine years. [33]
>
> I still had the curacy at Great Ness, going thither every Saturday after dinner and returning on Sunday evening, which was pleasant enough in the summer time, but inconvenient in the midst of winter, because at that season I was obliged to ride most of the way by night.[34]
>
> From Sir Edward Leighton of Loton I received a letter dated May 20 wherein it assured me that he has written to Lord Newport, on my behalf about the Curacy of Edstaston.[35]

As Samuel rode to Ness in July 1713, he observed and wrote in great detail about the celebrations for peace in almost every town; sheep roasting, and singing by the people, so great was the joy at the conclusion of the War of the Spanish Succession, which had been distinguished by the famous victories of the Duke of Marlborough. At the same time Mr Collier, the vicar of Great Ness, proposed certain terms by which he would resign the curacy of Edstaston to Samuel. Both then waited upon Lord Newport, at Mr Jobben's House near Shifnal to request a recommendation to Dr Chandler, and not long afterwards Samuel received a letter dated 25 November from Dr Chandler in Worcester, in which he declared, 'he was well pleased that Lord Newport and Lord Bradford both concurred in recommending a person for whom upon other accounts he had kind intentions, and that if Samuel acknowledged their favour in it, he and Samuel would never disagree'[36]

Samuel entered immediately upon the curacy of Edstaston, although he was paid from the preceding Michaelmas. However, Samuel admits that before leaving Ness he had contracted 'An intimate acquaintance with Mistress Edwards', who by letter sent him 'Intelligence of what passed in those parts'[37]

In 1714, he recorded that he was boarding at the school house, with his cousin Peter Edwards (who had also been educated at Donnington and at Christchurch College, Oxford) who had been elected the chief master of Wem school in September 1710. During Edward's time 'Great numbers of young gentlemen were bred under him'. He is described as being 'Politick, discreet, well bred with a majestic presence, being a big and comely man'.[38]

Marriage and Wem society
It just so happened that during school holidays, Samuel spent most of his

Edstaston Church, near Wem.

time at Great Ness, and it was there on 26 April 1714, at the age of seventy four, that Dorothy, the widow of John Edwards died, leaving all her personal effects and estate to her daughter Anna.

The Edwards family descended from the ancient Welsh stock of Lledrud,[39] claiming an illustrious pedigree, with ancestors such as Rhiryd Flaid, Lord of Pen Llyn in Merioneth; Meredith ap Bleyddyn, Prince of Powys, and Bleyddyn ap Cynan, King of Powys. Blood line was far more important in Wales than money or land. By the 17th century, at the time of his purchase of Great Ness, John Edwards could claim not only wealth and land but also a worthy pedigree. He had married Dorothy Barnes of The Low, Loppington and amongst their children was Anna, the youngest daughter, who was to become Samuel's wife.

Within three weeks of the death of Dorothy Edwards, on Whit Sunday 16 May 1714, Samuel and Anna were married at Baschurch Parish Church. It appears to have been a very sudden arrangement, for Samuel stated:

> I had not the least thought of matrimony when I went to Ness, and indeed it was not resolved or so much as mentioned till the evening before … As soon as Mr Hudson had given us his blessing we parted, my dear going back, and I with some danger getting back to Edstaston where I was to administer the sacrament … My wedding dinner happened to be worst I …[40]

The newly-weds were parted until the 11 June, when Samuel, together with his cousin Peter Edwards, went to meet, 'His dear spouse, who came that day to Wem. At the Crown, I provided a good dinner for the people attending the Eight Carts which carried all her goods.'[42] Losing no time and as 'quick off the mark, as ever', Samuel and Anna went to Shrewsbury on 23 June to prove the will of Dorothy Edwards.[41]

At this point it is illuminating to examine the history of Samuel's relationships with the fairer sex. On arrival at Great Ness, he had been accused of being too friendly with his landlady Mrs Wingfield of Alderton Hall, a widow, the mother of at least six children and his senior by some years. She had the income and security of a considerable estate, and this relationship was only ended on the intervention of her family. Then, within weeks of the death of Anna's mother, he is seen to marry an heiress immediately her fortune is announced. This, despite the fact that he made no secret of his opinion of the table the Edwards family kept, although he was very much aware of their social status, and that he had already admitted an intimate relationship with Anna during his earlier days at Great Ness.[42] The Edwards' were the principle family of Great Ness, having bought one of the largest estates in the parish from Captain John Smith in 1662.

By comparison, the Garbets of Walcot were in decline and their elevation to the rank of gentleman was not by descent but by reward. As previously stated the founder of the Garbet family was Robert Garbet of Acton Burnell, Salop, who was raised to the rank of gentleman because of his service to Henry V11; and from the settlement of the Acton Burnell estate, the Garbets acquired sizeable estates and remained within the ranks of the 'Petty Gentry'.[43]

The will of Francis Garbet, the vicar of Wroxeter, instructed his executor to pay 'Just £4 0s 0d to the poor of the parish'.[44] This will also mentions 'my sonne Baxter and his daughter Mary Baxter'[45] —could this 'sonne' have been Richard Baxter by adoption?

The next Garbet will, was that of Samuel Garbet born in 1624 in Wroxeter vicarage, and who died in 1710 at Norton, still in the parish of Wroxeter. His eldest son Francis, who had previously been settled on the Walcot estate by his father, was left in the will 'Just one bible, Samuel of Wem, his grandson, was left all his divinity books, his other grandchildren James and Elizabeth were bequeathed just two books apiece, all his other goods, cattle, chattels and estate he left to his youngest son Thomas, who was also sole executor'.[46] Although the Norton estate, which he left to his youngest son, was of considerable size, and Francis the eldest son had had the Walcot estate settled on him during his father's lifetime, the inventory of Samuel's personal effects and belongings appears to be paltry indeed, not that of a man who had purchased two sizeable estates. His books were valued at £5, one horse and two sheep at £6, bed furniture at £5, wearing apparel at £1 15s, and for 'Things not seen and forgotten', just five shillings. Just how much was 'Not seen and forgotten' could prove interesting, as Thomas , the sole executor and heir to his fathers estate, died in 1723 at the Norton estate, leaving an inventory which reveals a very comfortable lifestyle, a well furnished house, although no silver is listed. It lists household goods to the value of £80 and instruments of husbandry at £53 10s.[47] The will of Francis Garbet of Walcot was written on 26 March 1730, and leaves the residue of his personal estate to his dear wife Ann, and 'Revokes disannuls and makes void all former wills and testaments'.[48] Ann was also the sole executor, but pre-deceased her husband by some twelve months, dying in 1736.

James Garbet, the youngest son applied for probate, as the 'Lawful and administrator of all and singular goods, rights, credits, cattle and chattels of Francis Garbet, late of the parish of Wellington, dated 22nd April 1737'. This is interesting, because Samuel Garbet of Wem paid on at least three occasions, the sum of £100 to his father Francis Garbet, in anticipation of inheriting the estate, and his diary records that 'On January 30th 1737, the whole estate at Walcot fell to me on my father's death'.[49] However, by the 8 September 1738, James Garbet was obliged to write his own will and died the next day, leaving the whole estate to Samuel Garbet (junior) of Wem. This particular will, brought trouble to Samuel Garbet senior as Samuel Garbet junior refused to acknowledge the requests of his uncle James in respect of payments to the poor of St Alkmund's parish. His father Samuel, in defence of his son, stated that his brother's estate* would not realise enough cash to cover the requests, and reminded the Rev John Cotton, vicar of St Alkmund's, that the wardens of the said parish had refused to honour the bills of James Garbet for the charges in his account book for 'the physyc to the poor of the parish'.

Though each of the last generation of Garbets left sizeable estates, details of their personal goods and actual cash in hand in comparison with that of the Edward's family appear paltry indeed.

In contrast, inventories of the Edwards' estate of Great Ness inform us that their family had more disposable income and far more worldly goods. When John Edwards senior, of Great Ness, father of Anna, Samuel's wife, wrote his last will and testament on 22 September 1708 — some five months before his death — he could have hardly envisaged the problems and trouble caused, or the time taken for the executors to settle his accounts. Having previously settled messuages and lands upon his two eldest sons (John and Robert) and an unknown sum on his youngest son (Richard) who had emigrated to Virginia. Internal family squabbles continued for more than twenty years, with continual threats of court action.

He bequeathed to Anna £250, which was laid out in a mortgage of £300, legacies of £10 to two nieces and £100 to his grandaughter Katherine Derwas. To his wife Dorothy, he left one half of his silver plate and household goods — with the exception of his silver tankard (given to him by Lord Bridgewater, the Lord of the Manor of Ness Strange) which he gave to his eldest son John, to remain in his dwelling house. The other half of his household goods, all cattle and chattels, was left to his executors towards the payment of his just debts and legacies. It was this simple section of the will, that was to cause so much trouble over the years to come.

His executors were his son Robert and son-in-law William Watkins (of the parish of Myddle) and they produced numerous inventories of all his goods, chattels and assets. Over the years, both of them were accused of falsifying

---

* It would appear that the property of James Garbet included two 'very genteel' houses in Shrewsbury High Street (worth at least £450) and the contents of the house and shop. At the time of his death, he was owed considerable amounts of money.

the accounts, and to confuse matters further, when Robert Edwards died in 1725, his widow and sole executor, Elizabeth Edwards refused demands that she should disclose the accounts of her husband appertaining to his father's will. However, following these disputes, various inventories and accounts were produced which enabled an assessment of John Edwards' estate to be made.

Most of the demands were instigated by Samuel Garbet of Wem, who had to pay the sum of £20 for a restitution bond, in order that he could receive his wife's inheritance. He also queried if he 'Samuel Garbet, should be concerned in the funeral charges and other expenses subsequent to the testators death, there being debts due, and owing to him at his decease'.[50] He also questioned 'Whether the executors be not obliged, before they demand restitution, to give me a particular account of the full profits they have received from the goods and personal estate over and above what they were appraised at'.[51] It was these queries that eventually produced the details which revealed the full inventories of John Edwards' estate which were appraised on 24 February 1709 and amounted to £274-17s-11d plus debts of £345 due to the deceased. Then, within a year of the testators death, the executors received a total of £414-8s-5d from interests accruing on mortgages, rents and cattle and corn sold from the barn. The executors admitted to a total of £652 but stood accused of omitting £264-17s-1d, plus a further £60 in cash. Rents and lease money produced £977 over and above the value of messuages and lands previously bequeathed to John and Robert Edwards.[52]

Probate inventories, which are lists of moveable goods formerly belonging to deceased people exclude other freehold or copyhold land. They were valued, after death, on oath by neighbours and executors as part of the process of obtaining probate. Most are reasonably complete and accurate and provide the historian with an invaluable source of information on the material environment of the lives of ordinary people. They are also useful in that they can also give details of the number and type of rooms within the deceased's house.

The details and papers appertaining to the Edwards' family and their estates in Great Ness, leaves one in no doubt that the family had a comfortable and well-furnished home, and an estate that supported three sons and their families. The inventories of Francis Garbet of Walcot (1737) and John Edwards of Great Ness (1709) appear at first sight to be straight forward, and indeed were verified for probate. However, closer inspection reveals that Francis Garbet, had far more goods and chattels than were listed[53] and that the inventory of John Edwards recorded just £25 cash in the house. Cross referencing with the Edwards papers reveal that on the 13 November 1727, one John Bolas, swore before magistrates that he had heard 'Mr William Watkins, one of the executors of John Edward's will, declare in the house of Mr Francis Chambre, Attorney at Law of Petton, 'That Mr John Edwards late of Great Ness, left goods and chattels and personal estate sufficient to pay off all his just debts and legacies, with some hundreds of pounds to spare'.'[54] Watkins also admitted that fifty thraves of winter corn in the barn, together with several other things of considerable value, were not appraised, and that several thraves of growing corn, wheat, muncorn and rye were under-valued and that a lease worth £30 *per annum* in the inventory did bring in £10 *per annum* clear above the reserved rent and taxes, and had done so yearly, since the testators death.[55]

With such evidence, one can understand why Samuel Garbet questioned the actions of the executors of his father-in-law's will, especially when he had to pay £20 for a restitution bond in order to receive his wife's legacy. This still left him with a liability in having to pay towards other legacies, especially with regard to the 'Virginia Affair',[56] an account the executors appeared very reluctant to settle and which was not paid until 1727. This concerned the marriage portion, which comprised a note for the sum of some £300 on Mary the eldest daughter of John and Dorothy Edwards, when she married George Joynson, for the use of herself or her heirs. There appeared to be some difficulty in the payment of this bond, so Mary joined with her husband in a chancery suite for the recovery of this amount. The case highlighted the fact that a sum of £162-15s was still unpaid and that the court allowed John Edwards (junior) £50-13s-4d for his charges. This reduced the principle sum to £112-1s-8d, and this was ordered at interest. Mary Joynson died in childbirth and her only daughter, also named Mary, was married in 1721 to Charles Tomkiss, apothecary and surgeon, born in Oswestry, but then living in the colony of Virginia. In 1724 Joynson, Tomkiss and his wife Mary gave power of attorney to Miciah Perry and Nathanial Edwards, two London merchants, to demand the remaining part of Mrs Joynson's fortune, which by then had computed to a sum of some £400. A bill is said to have been filed —although with no apparent success— but the executors still refused to settle the affair. In 1727, Tomkiss arrived in England and subpoenaed the executors of John Edwards to appear in Chancery. By letter he indicated he would accept £165 in settlement and the executors then offered him £112 which, at first, he refused to accept.

The executors had paid out none of the legacies unless there was a restitution bond involved. All this became a great worry to Samuel Garbet, especially after he had paid £20 in order to receive his wife's legacy and

White Horse, Wem.

more cover money paid by his mother-in-law, in order that they might recover goods from the inventory. With Robert Edwards now dead and his executrix only acknowledging debts which could be proved upon her, and with matters having been transacted in such a manner that it was not always possible to carry the proof far enough, Samuel was in danger of having to refund the £300 of his wife's legacy, or of having to maintain a chancery suite against the executors, which might cost much more, and last as long as he might live. Samuel records, 'This was the greatest misfortune that ever befell me, it gave me more uneasiness and vexation than all the other cross accidents of my life put together'.[57]

Samuel must have decided that near twenty years was too long a time to settle the last will and testament of John Edwards, and from letters and accounts we witness a new side of Samuel's nature. He invited Charles Tomkiss to Wem, and played the mediator between all the parties. 'Tis true I have laboured heartily to bring you and them to an accommodation, and I hope I have not laboured in vain' [58] he wrote to Charles Tomkiss, signing the letter 'Your affectionate kinsman'

In 1727, Charles Tomkiss finally accepted the sum of £112, thus bringing the 'Virginia Affair' to a close, after which Samuel writes that 'Thus far I have communicated your proposals to them, and their answer to you' — though one letter states that he, Samuel, sent a copy of one of Tomkiss's letters to Mr Watkins' executor, and quaintly stated 'Omitting only that part, which you desired might be Under the Rose'.[59] Is this an indication of a leaning by Samuel to the Jacobite cause of 1715? Many of his gentry neighbours are recorded as being members of the Jacobite Cycle of the White Rose Club, which met at the Wynnstay Hotel in Wrexham. These meetings raised eyebrows as far afield as London. Jacobite songs and ditties could be heard all over the town, as the members toasted 'The King over the water'. Samuel goes on to wish 'That they (the executors) had afforded somewhat more handsome and more agreeable to your generous temper, but money is what few people can easily bring themselves to part with! even when it apparently does not belong to them'.[60]

The Garbets settle in Wem
Samuel welcomed his bride to Wem on 11 June 1714, almost a month after their wedding, together with her eight wagons of goods and chattels.* Most of these were the items of property left to Dorothy, the relict of John Edwards of Great Ness, many of which appear both in the inventories of Samuel Garbet senior (1756) and of Samuel Garbet junior (1774).[61] Amongst the goods listed are: 'The clock in the Japanned Case, the Red Leather Chairs, tables, beds and every item required in the kitchen'.[62]

Samuel and Anna settled into Wem society.[63] His pocket book[64] informs us that he moved into a house where he paid a rental £5 *per annum*, payable half yearly. This appears to have been on a three-year lease from Robert Sandiland. This move was never anything more than a short term provision, for on 16 June 1715 Samuel paid Richard Lyth of Uppington £80 'for my Burgage and land belonging thereto in Wem, John Pigeon, one of the bailiffs of the town gave me seison (or Possession) this was my first purchace'.[65]

The exact location of Samuel Garbets burgage plot in New Street[66] —and that of the house he rented from Robert Sandiland— has been difficult to establish because at some time in the past all the documents that might have given any clue to the actual address have been mutilated; pages have been torn from pocket books, addresses snipped from letter headings and maps have been likewise censured. His personal documents relating to the property in New Street fail to pinpoint the exact location of his house. It is unfortunate his *History of Wem* did not include a detailed map of the town of Wem, this is probably because the first publication was in 1818 some sixty years after Samuel's death. The lack of maps is all the more puzzling because

St. Peter & St. Paul's Parish Church, Wem.

Samuel did execute a number of maps of the town, including some excellent examples of early cartographic work. The main maps drawn during Samuel's lifetime depict every burgage plot in the town, though the list of names associated with them are those of the 17th century occupiers.[67] Unfortunately, the only map including the names of his contemporaries is incomplete, and that portion which includes the New Street area is missing.[68]

His first recorded home in Wem, may have been the house listed by Iris Woodward in *The Story of Wem*, as Sandilands House, which she believed was number 59 Noble Street, built on the site of the Civil War prison.[69] Garbet himself refers to this house as being used during the Civil War, and that it was later owned by the Sandilands. However, we know the Sandiland family owned more than one property in Wem, including a burgage plot in High Street, which Garbet later bought, and that they also had an interest in a burgage in New Street. It would appear though, that Noble Street is the most likely location of Samuel's house, for it was known that the house on this site was used by previous school masters of Wem Free School.

It was in Sandilands House that Samuel Garbet junior was born, a little before midnight on 21 June 1716. This event was recorded briefly in Samuel's note book — although he allocated more space for details concerning the construction of a new brewhouse. It is, however, significant that within the collection of documents there are no less than three letters of congratulations on the safe delivery of a son, from Anna's brothers, 'Hoping that the little boy will bring great pleasure to you both'.[70] There are no surviving congratulatory letters from the Garbet family on this most important event.

Samuel states in *The History of Wem*, that he owned four burgage plots in New Street, two of which were freehold. Together with the tantalising comment, 'That the house wherein I now live, once stood at Edstaston. After the fire of 1677 it received four or five families. When it came into my hands, was framed anew, and made a convenient dwelling'.[71]

Various clues within the collection of papers would suggest that the Old Hall in New Street was the Garbet house but there is no other evidence to support this. On the contrary, local belief is that this house was built in 1725 for the Dickins family. It is thought that there was once a timber-framed house further down New Street, which was later incorporated into the row of houses now known as Islington Crescent. Detailed and careful accounts kept by Samuel indicate features that wholly concern building costs, many of the letters kept in the Garbet papers are just as meticulous.[72]

It is acknowledged that 'Black and White' architecture was the hallmark of the west midlands and occurred throughout the region; and this 'Highly individual character was in the main due to the geological consistency of the sandstone and clay of the low lying areas, which gave rise in the past to dense oakwoods.'[73] It would appear that what the builders did, was in fact, common practice, the re-use of an existing timber frame which was re-erected on a new site, the infill being made with 18th century brick, replacing where necessary the earlier wattle and daub. There were two distinct types of house framing:

1. Closely set uprights divided by traverse beams.
2. Framing in large panels. Generally speaking the Worcester and Hereford districts have wider panelling whilst Shropshire, Cheshire and parts of Lancashire the close set studding.[74]

The work on Samuel's residence was definitely of the latter type.

We can now witness another facet of Samuel's character by studying the careful, meticulous and dated accounts kept by him with regard to the construction of this house.[75] Again, in his green note book he states 'The charge of my dwelling house, Brewhouse, and the Fiddlers House amounted to £127-0s-0d'.[76] The first payments occur in 1716 and were for the delivery of bricks, tiles, lime and laths to the site. In 1717 he paid 1s-4d for sinking the cellar, 5 shillings for making the cellar walls, and 1 shilling for paving the

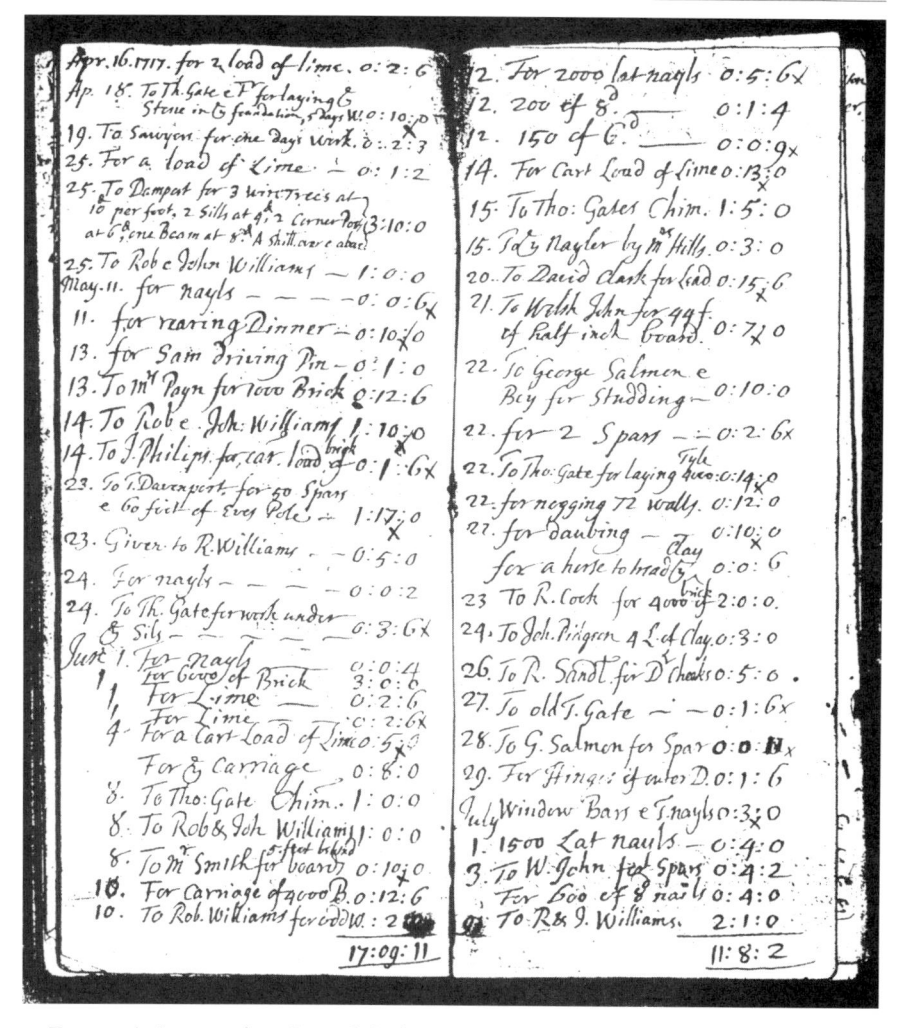

Two specimin pages from Samuel Garbet's notebook covering the dates April 16, 1717 — June 1, 1717. Most of the entris relate to the building costs of his house.

floor. He also paid 10 shillings for a 'Rearing dinner' no doubt when the frame was 'Upright'. In total some 23,000 bricks, 15,000 tiles (together with some architectural dressed stone) were used and a new well was sunk at a cost of £1–6s (which included 80 feet of stonework).[77] The most interesting items are those for the 'nogging , studding and glazing' which indicate the construction of a sizeable timber framed house. These items, together with a further order of 2,000 bricks and coping stones for the building of the wall before the house, appear to fit the pattern of the house and garden of 'Old Hall'.

Other entries include the payment of £2 to Thomas Gate, a builder, which was 10 shillings too much. In February 1717 he paid Samuel Sadler 5s–6d which was 1 penny over for want of change, and on 12 July 1717, a delivery of some 300 feet of board was, according to Samuel's reckoning, some 10 feet short. He must also have been thought of as something of a 'soft touch' by the children of Wem, for his accounts are peppered with items for 6d and 4d to the children for help in unloading goods.[78]

An entry in one of Samuel's notebooks, dated 30 August 1717, states 'I received £250:0:0, part of my wife's portion' and then 'This summer I built my house in New Street, and on September 3rd removed to it'.[79] Samuel Garbet was now well settled in the town of Wem, father of a young son, with a wife of good family connections and his own well furnished home in New Street, which placed him in the 'Top Drawer' of town society. He had been second master at Wem Free School since 1712, and curate of Edsaston Chapel, Wem Parish, since 1713.

When the new rector of Wem, Mr Eyton was appointed, he resolved to do the duty of the church himself, 'But would have me read prayers there every third week!, tho this was a great imposition, yet for peace sake it was complied with for many years'.[80]

Despite all this, it appears that Samuel was still unsettled for he writes in 1716 that his old school master Mr Markham had died, 'tis probable I might have succeeded him in the school at Donnington, with the Donotive of Uppington worth £70:0:0 per annum, if I had made the least application, though I was inclined to tug at it, I thought myself well provided for at Wem'.[81] He also wrote to Mr Kynaston about the vicarage of Ryton and received in reply a letter dated 19 January 1717.

> Dear Sir,
> You have not only my hand, but my heart in all sincerity, no one shall more sincerely level at your interest, or rather my own than your old, but true friend ...
> Wm Kynaston.

Samuel recalls that 'Not withstanding, these warm professions', he procured the living for Mr Jefferys, whose uncle, as was reported, had presented him with a purse of guineas.[82] This was just one of the many applications made by Garbet for a parish of his own, but his refusal to solicit votes for would be patrons and his strong independence resulted in the many refusals.

David Hey states in *An English Rural Cumminity, Myddle:* 'That one's role and standing in the parish still depended upon the amount of property one possessed'.[83] There is no doubt that Samuel was obviously of the same opinion because, as he moved into his newly bought burgage in New Street, he also started to buy the many properties and estates that were held in his name when he died.

On 22 November 1717 he purchased from Mr John Goodale of Nantwich, 'The Great Shaws' for £115, 'Which I paid in guineas, then passing at 21s-6d, but nine days after was reduced to 21s-0d'.[84] This estate amounted to about 110 acres, which he immediately let to Rowland Weaver for the sum of £7 *per annum*. Today, there is no known house associated with this land, only pasture and woodland known as the 'Shaws', but soon after the purchase Samuel paid builders to replace the four hearths and to re-flag the floors of the Great Shaws.[85] The bill for this work was signed by Rowland Weaver, then the tenant.

There then followed a series of purchases, enhancing Samuel's status within the locality.

1728 — He purchased from Mr John Whitefield, the Middle Fields and Barns Croft for the sum of £190, it being copyhold land.[86]

1737 — On the 30 January, 'The whole estate at Walcot fell to me'. This was leased to Mr Hazlehurst, Ironmaster, for £57 per annum. He also bought a freehold field from Mrs Higginson for £84[87] and laid out a further £90 by way of mortgages on her two town houses in Wem.[88]

1738 — Samuel lent Roger Dyers £100 upon the mortgage and lands in Wem.[89] The property in High Street was later rented from Sam junior by Thomas Wilkinson, a long term tenant of this property and it is recorded that as well as the house, there was a stable, a cow house, a barn of three bays, a hempyard, a small garden and a large garden; also six parcels of land in the township of Wem — three arable fields known by the names of Hughes' field, Great Middle fields, and lesser Middle fields.

1742 — He purchased off Richard Cooper, Cranmore Croft [Creamore] for £60.[90]

1743 — On the 2 February, he bought from George Walford, two freehold messuages and tenements in Wem for £55.[91] On the 16 April he also bought two copyhold messuages and tenements for £140 from Mr William Price.[92]

1744 — He bought Crabtree Crofts from Mr John Sheton, for £100 (plus

the court fees and fines) — this was copyhold land.[93]
1748 — He now made his final and most expensive purchase, buying the Newtown Estate for the sum £1,400.[94] This comprised of the messuage in Newtown, the Higher Croft, the yard by the house, Kenwricks Meadow now divided into Caulder Croft, Round Hill, Jamma Croft, Ditches Croft, Colebrook (said to be Colebreck) Hill Leasow, Poole Meadow (chopped meadow), the Marle Leasows and the new erected messuage in Wolverly. Also the following lands in Newtown:

The Upper Hoyes	5a	1r	28p
Manings Yard		2r	35p
The Garden		2r	5p
The Little Croft		1r	14p

Samuel records that, in order to pay for such a large estate, he was obliged to sell Crabtree Croft, and call in all bonds, mortgages and debts. The Crown Inn at Wem was appointed for the time and place of payment on 6 June 1748. The money was counted (cash), there was a dispute over the measures and boundaries and finally the money was paid and the deeds signed and delivered up to Samuel with all the writings of the Newtown Estate. This was the last entry written by Samuel Garbet in his diary, some nine years before his death.

Over a period of nearly thirty years, therefore, Samuel Garbet spent a total of £2,600 plus court fees and fines) buying a total of nineteen properties in and around Wem. The list of tenants (of both Samuel Garbet senior and junior) is:

William Hazlehurst	Elizabeth Reeves
Thomas Wilkinson	Thomas Corbet
Sam Colcot	John Davies
Andrew Harries	Mary Wright
Sam Groom	Frances Williams
Edward Elkes	Mary Millington
Thomas Corbet	John Besford
Sam Forgham	Thomas Millington
C. Watkins	Rachel Besford
James Forgham	Mary Bagshaw
William Higginson	Elizabeth Boroughs
William Wycherly	Sam Forgham
William Price	Roger Dyos
Joseph Chace	Richard Astley
Richard Huffah	Mr Henshaw, Walcot.

George Fardell	Andrew Moris
John Paulett	Mr Cooper
Chris Watkins	Charles Murr
Sam Griffith	William Wilkinson
John Chidlow	Rowland Weaver
Samuel Walmsly	Mr Tyler
Thomas Corbet	

In order to determine the means by which these purchases were made, it is necessary to examine Samuel's income which provided the monies to make them possible.

His house was furnished with the contents of the eight wagon loads of goods and chattels brought by his wife from Great Ness. However, it is not known how much cash in hand Anna brought with her, but we know that they received her marriage settlement of £250. In 1717, Samuel's own income was £30 *per annum* from his curacy at Edstaston, plus as he states 'The great tithes of Edstaston and Cotton, for servicing the curacy, they are now set at £74 per annum'.[95] He had been elected second master at Wem Grammar School on the 11 March 1712, though he did not actually begin teaching until Lady Day — some three years before his marriage. There is nothing in any of his papers, nor in the extended accounts of Wem Grammar School, to indicate the level of his salary as a schoolmaster. We do know, however, that Thomas Adams, the founder of Wem Free school, left estates in Northwood and Edstaston, both in the parish of Wem, to the value of £285 *per annum*. This sum was considered to be insufficient to maintain the Head, second and third masters of the school, and the feofees were instructed to augment this income by contributions from others.[96] Within the Garbet manuscripts are three papers[97] which appear to be answers to queries about Shrewsbury Grammar School, details and dates of the foundation and more importantly, details of the masters' salaries. These state that the headmaster was in receipt of £60 *per annum*, plus a further £20 *per annum* for teaching the catechism. The second master received a total of £45 *per annum*, the third master £30. All these figures correspond to those quoted by Mingay, for he tells of a certain 'Mr John Fuller a prominent Sussex Ironmaster, who engaged the services of a Mr Bear, a clergyman, who specialized in private tuition, at a fee of fifty guineas per annum per pupil, for board and tuition'.[98]

Samuel's income fluctuated from year to year, rising from £139 *per annum* to a peak of £392, and his average yearly income computes out at £250. This

level of income would have placed Samuel Garbet amongst the wealthiest of Wem society.
According to King and Colequin,

> The average income of a freeholder during the 18th century was from, £84 to £200 for the better freeholder. and from £50 to £90 for lesser freeholders. King thought that lesser freeholders earned a little more than the average income of farmers. But Colequin reversed this judgement, putting the farmers income at £120 as compared with the lesser freeholders £90.[99]

But monied wealth alone was not enough at either village or county level. It appears that land was necessary to the social climber in village society as was money to the merchant. Land was not the only type of property, but it was supreme, more stable than merchants' stock-in-trade and more valuable than industrial implements, but in compensation, income from land tended to confer higher social status on its owner than an equivalent income from any other source.[100]

Amongst the clergy, one of the largest professional groups, there were considerable differences in lifestyle. By the end of Elizabeth I's reign, the great majority of beneficed men had taken wives, for married men were more likely to have their household run efficiently and were therefore able to fulfil their duty of hospitality. Well remunerated clergy were able to devote themselves to prayer, preaching and pastoral work.

Samuel was fortunate in having married well, with Anna able to offer hospitality (hopefully improved form that at Great Ness). They enjoyed a place within the local social scene. His inventory tells us that he enjoyed the use of silver tableware, fine china, damask tablecloths and napkins, silver salts, also a gun and a brace of pistols, looking glasses, paintings, mahogany furniture and plenty of delftware.[101] His personal wearing apparel were kept in the room over the kitchen, the warmest bedroom, amongst the lists were frock buckles, knee buckles shoe buckles and sleeve buckles, all of silver. On his feather bed are listed two quilts and two blankets — an appraisal that was made in August! Gowns and wearing apparel were listed at £6 6s, with three hair brushes and five sweetmeat glasses. Books and maps were listed at over £60. The whole was appraised by John Wickstead and Samuel Pigeon.

It is clear, that with the ability to save money and invest in property, Samuel was living well within his income. His pocket book tells us that he employed live-in maids, for with up to ten boys boarding with him, extra help would have been required. His payments to people seeking charity at his door, although the individual amounts were small (3d, 6d or a 1s), could mount up as he frequently had two or three visitors each week. Also recorded are occasional payments for day labouring in the garden: 1 day's weeding 5d, 4 day's weeding 1s 8d, 1s to cut hedges, 6d for seeds, 8d for peas, 8d for plants, 2d for spinage 2d for parsley, 6d for seeds 1s 6d for a bundle of spars 2d for onion seeds 3d for kidney beans.[102]

One group of papers in the collection, perhaps the most interesting of all, comprise entirely of his bills and accounts, which reveal in great detail the hidden evidence of his daily life. These documents confirm that Samuel had a preference for the good things in life. We already know of his liking for good food and from these pages can deduce that he must have been one of the best dressed men in Wem; with clothes and suits made from fine damask, best broadcloth, best greycloth, mohair, silk and velvets.

Though Samuel was fond of giving amusing anecdotal pen pictures of his contemporaries and family, of himself he is completely silent. Yet from his accounts one can imagine him as a well dressed man of his day, possibly a little on the stout side. If you calculate the amount of material which was required to make his attire, we find that 5 yards of broadcloth are needed for a jacket, 10 yards for a pair of knee length breeches, and some 9 to 10 yards of cloth for a night gown, and a later bill quotes no less than 18 yards for a similar garment.[103]

If one compares the amounts shown on his bills for food, all of which include large amounts of sugar, together with regular quantities of cinnamon, cloves, mixed spices, currants and raisins, one can assume that someone in the household had a very sweet tooth.[104] Many of the bills do not appear to be complete, and, in the main, they are from tailors, grocers and booksellers. Yet every one is signed by the supplier as paid in full. All bills state this, thus we can assume that Samuel did not approve of being in debt.

Every item is listed, from different types of cloth, linings, buttons, threads, *etc*, and Samuel has indented each bill with what the items were for *e.g.* 'Sam's Riding Coat', 'My nightgown', 'My Breeches' and 'Short cassock'.[105] As keen as ever, he noted whenever he felt that he had been overcharged, 'Calimo was for a gown, it ought to have been charged at 17s-0d per yard not 18s-0d,[106] ... 8 yards of fine silk damask at 2s-0d a yard, with silk thread 5d, for a short cassock'. With reference to this latter item, he comments, 'Is 8 yards full enough?, 7^{1}/2 might do!'[107] He was willing to sacrifice half-a-yard of material for the sake of saving a shilling! Though he always paid his accounts on demand, he always expected a discount for doing so,[108] e.g. for a bill totalling £2-15s-3d, signed off as having been received in full,he writes 'paid £2-14-6', a discount of nine pence.

The vegetables for the house came from his 'Beloved Garden', but there are still items not listed, of flour there is no mention, though this would have been bought by the sack from the local mill, meat is only mentioned but once, 'Dec 19th 1745, had off Peter Pidgeon a flank of beef at 40lb, which at 2d per lb came to 6s 8d, had also a sirloin 29lb which at 2d per lb comes to 6s 0d, 2lb of stakes 4d'.[109] Of hats and shoes there is no mention, other than those he bought for his pupils.

However, Samuel spent a great deal of money on books on a wide variety of subjects: divinity, classical history, poetry, law and the latest maps by 'Dr Wells, drawn on very fine paper', Jewish history, Milton's *Paradise Lost*, *Travels in Turkey*, Latin and Greek primers and grammars, together with many of the new county histories then being published. Of all his books, his favourite was *Britannica Depicted* (or *Ogilby Improved*), by John Owen of the Middle Temple, which is a survey of the roads and distances, accounts of all cities, towns and boroughs with arms, antiquarian charters, trades along with descriptions of streets in each county. He says of this neat pocket book, 'One page in this book contains more remarks than any whole book yet published.'[110] Though Samuel's taste was catholic, the bulk of his buys were in the field of topography and history, and he records his love of pocket sized histories.

With regard to the property he owned Samuel was not blind to the need for repairs. At Walcot, the repairs started just after he inherited the estate from his father in 1738. 'Allowed meat and lodgings for the carpenters also for the Thatcher, £7-8-0. Smith's work and paviors, sinking new wells or cleaning the well, which was frequent'. Rebuilding the stables over a period of ten years (1738–49), he spent £37-16s-11d. Between 1749 and 1756 he had the gates renewed, relayed the barn floor, new sills and nogging on the stable wall.[111] He renewed the lease of Walcot to William Hazlehurst, ironmaster. On 1 November 1757, there is an article of agreement between Samuel Garbet of Wem and Joshua Gee of Tearn in the parish of Atcham, ironmaster '... for selling all cordwood trees marked in his estate lying and being at Walcot in the parish of Wellington. 5s 9d for each and every statute cordwood that shall arise out and from the said wood ... and a sufficient place shall be found for the coaling of the said wood ... and poles shall be provided for cabins for the workmen ...'. The agreement is also signed by 'William Hazlehurst, Ironmaster'.

At the Newtown estate (bought in 1748), he spent money on re-thatching, re-glazing, new gutter tiles, new lead pump, carts for lime, 4,000 tiles, 106 gutters, gates, and a new roof for the pig sty. The chimney was also repaired at a cost of £27-5s-10d.[112]

All the properties bought by Samuel received attention: for retiling, thatching, floors relaid, *etc*. There is no doubt that judging by the entries in his pocket note books, he was a good landlord. Always, on the receipt of rents due, he allowed tenants for the money they had spent on their houses, and always returned an 'earnest' of 2s or 2s-6d. Also listed in the accounts are the land taxes made for Wem and Walcot:

1745, Wem
Land Taxes at 4s 0d in the pound, made in quarterly payments.

My Dwelling house	£2-3s.
Higgins Field	£1-4s-2d.
Walfords House	£1-0s-1d.
Wm Prices House	£1-2s-1d.
Middle Field & Barns Croft	£2-10s-1d.
Coopers House & Creamore Croft	£3-1s-0d.

He also made payments to the parish surveyor, '2 shillings for a man to perform a days work on the highway' — every member of the parish had to work for up to four days each year (later six days), or pay someone else to work for them.

Also listed in detail, are payments for the poor levy which amounted to 5s-6d a quarter. He was also very careful in listing his highway levy, his church levy and for 'Window Taxes' — in 1748 he paid half yearly on Lady Day and Michaelmas, 4s-6d a half year, 9s-0d a full year, that is, 2s-0d for the house and 6d a piece for 14 windows, and to open two further windows the tax would have risen to 14 shillings, viz 2 shillings for the house and 9d apiece for 16 windows.[113]

The Schoolmaster
Samuel's time was, in the main, divided between the church and the school. When he first arrived in the town as second master in 1712 the school was nearly empty, yet it was soon to fill up.[114] As can be seen from the statistics printed below, there was a gradual increase in the numbers of both day scholars and boarders.

The Free School in Wem as it was originally called, was founded in 1650 by Sir Thomas Adams and was situated in Noble Street. At the time of its foundation it was the only Shropshire grammar school and employed three masters. It was free to the sons of parishoners (apart from a small admission fee of between 7s-6d and 10s, plus a 1d payment for sweeping the school). Nonconformists were not excluded.

Numbers of pupils at Wem Grammar School

Day Boys	Boarders
1715 — 8	1716 — 1
1716 — 15	1717 — 2
1717 — 20	1718 — 3
1718 — 20	1719 — 3
1719 — 14	1720 — 3
1720 — 12	1721 — 3
1721 — 9	1722 — 4
1722 — 16	1723 — 4
1723 — 12	1724 — 4
1724 — 11	1725 — 4
1725 — 13	1726 — 3
1726 — 10	1727 — 3
1727 — 11	1728 — 2
1728 — 7	1729 — ?
1729 — 3	1730 — ?
1730 — 4	1731 — 1
1731 — 11	1732 — 2
1732 — 16	1733 — 5
1733 — 22	1734 — 7
1734 — 27	1735 — 7

Schoolmasters salaries varied from area to area during that period, but there does appear to be a near standard rate for county grammar schools. This, during the period 1712–50 was between £30 and £50 *per annum*. We do know that in 1824 the second master received £70 per annum, so if we take the lower rate of £30 as being the equivalent to his curate's salary, we can begin to work out his total income. This was also supplemented by the annual fees paid by his scholars, plus also the fees paid by those boarders who stayed in his house.

These fees, as with all his accounts are meticulously recorded within his notebooks, mainly notebook No 6, although they are interspersed with other items. The fees remained constant for many years at £1 for schooling, plus £10–12 *per annum* for boarding.[115] Thankfully, because of these itemised accounts, one can visualise life in Wem as a boy boarder with Samuel Garbet. During the summer months (March to September) they had to be in school by 6*a.m.*, lunch was from 11*a.m.* to 1*p.m.* and then further lessons until 5*p.m.*

```
                           School.                    Corkpence

     1st head class    Dan: Payne
        1719.          Rich. Manlove — fm Leppington
                       Roger Trevor ⊙ eldest Son of Roger Trevor
                                      of Bodinyvel
                       Tho: Trevor Vic: of Cissifty
                       John Pryce .   10
                       John Chettoe
                       ─────────────────────────────

     His head Class    John Howard
        1720.          Rich. Davies (son of .... of Trewylan.)
                       Bennet Dorfet  ⊙ /
                       Tho. Vaughan - of ye Wood. ⊙
                       Sam. Barnes, ye Clerk's Son. ⊙
                       Tho. Payne. (of Noneley.)
                       ─────────────────────────────

     His head Class    Franc: Astley ⊙.
        1721.          Rich. Lawrence Vicar of ...... , Kent
                       Geo. Tyler (Pepperhill
  Jane Chaddock went ) Jame's Lowe
       away 1720.    ) Edw. Best.
                       ─────────────────────────────

     Head Class        Rich. Pigeon.
        1722.          Tho: Tyler _ 5.
  Sam: Barnes          Joseph Swanwick
  James Forgham        Benj. Wingfield,(Minister of St Mary's Salop)
  D. Tho: Barnes -     Robt Davies. 3.  ⊙ 1748. of Tilley.
      went away 1721.
```

A section from the class lists of Wem Grammar School contained in the Garbet Papers.

Pupils had leave to play on one day a fortnight. There was three weeks holiday at Christmas and Easter, but there is no mention of any summer holidays, indeed there are many entries in the school accounts covering the months of July and August.[116]

Discipline was strict, and one could be expelled for any of the following offences, swearing, cursing, taking the Lord's name in vain, stealing, lying, filthy talk, gaming, tippling, quarrelling and drunkenness. Despite this, only one boy was sent down, 'Benjamin Stone, turned away on the 7th July 1733, after just three weeks'.[117]

Each boy was allowed 1 penny in pocket money every Saturday, but they also had to pay, 1 penny per term for sweeping of the school, 1 penny to the barber for hair-cutting, 2 pence for ink and papers, 6 pence for coals against the winter cold and 6 pence for bloodletting. New gloves cost £1, mending a pair of shoes 7 pence, buttons 2 pence and a hat 5 shillings. However, it was not all doom and gloom for the scholars, for Samuel would often pay 3 pence for them to see a 'Shew'. All these extras were billed to the parents at the end of each term.[118]

Although many clergymen had to turn to teaching as a means of supplementing their inadequate stipends, many of the masters of 18th century free grammar schools and the rising public schools, were making a very real place for themselves within their local society.[119] The decline of the public grammar school was mainly due to a lack of adequate supervision, an inflexible curriculum, poor teaching and a mix of boys from different social groupings. However, a large proportion of the scholars, perhaps half or even more, were the sons of clergymen, professional men, merchants and craftsmen, small traders and farmers.[120] Asa Briggs states 'That opportunities for education depended directly on social rank, yet even the upper class education was often haphazard, and there was lively debate as to whether the poor should be educated at all!'[121]

It is clear when reading Samuel's pocket books and notes, that he was in favour of education for all. All his accounts except one, were strictly cash, the exception being John Randell, who started at Wem Free School on 24 December 1724. His father is listed as a nailer, and it is evident from the accounts that he paid Samuel in kind, for we find in one of the notebooks the following entries:

> April 2nd 1725, rec 300 of 8d nails and a 100 of 6d nails, August 1725, rec 200 of 8d nails, 100 of 6d and a 100 of 2d, Jan 1727 rec 5s-0d in nails.'[122]

* *Wem parish registers record a marriage on Dec 12th 1714 of John Randell to Elizabeth Pay, and on 13 December 1715 'John son of John Randell, Nailer and Elizabeth baptised.'[123]*

Reverend Sr   Apr 17 1716

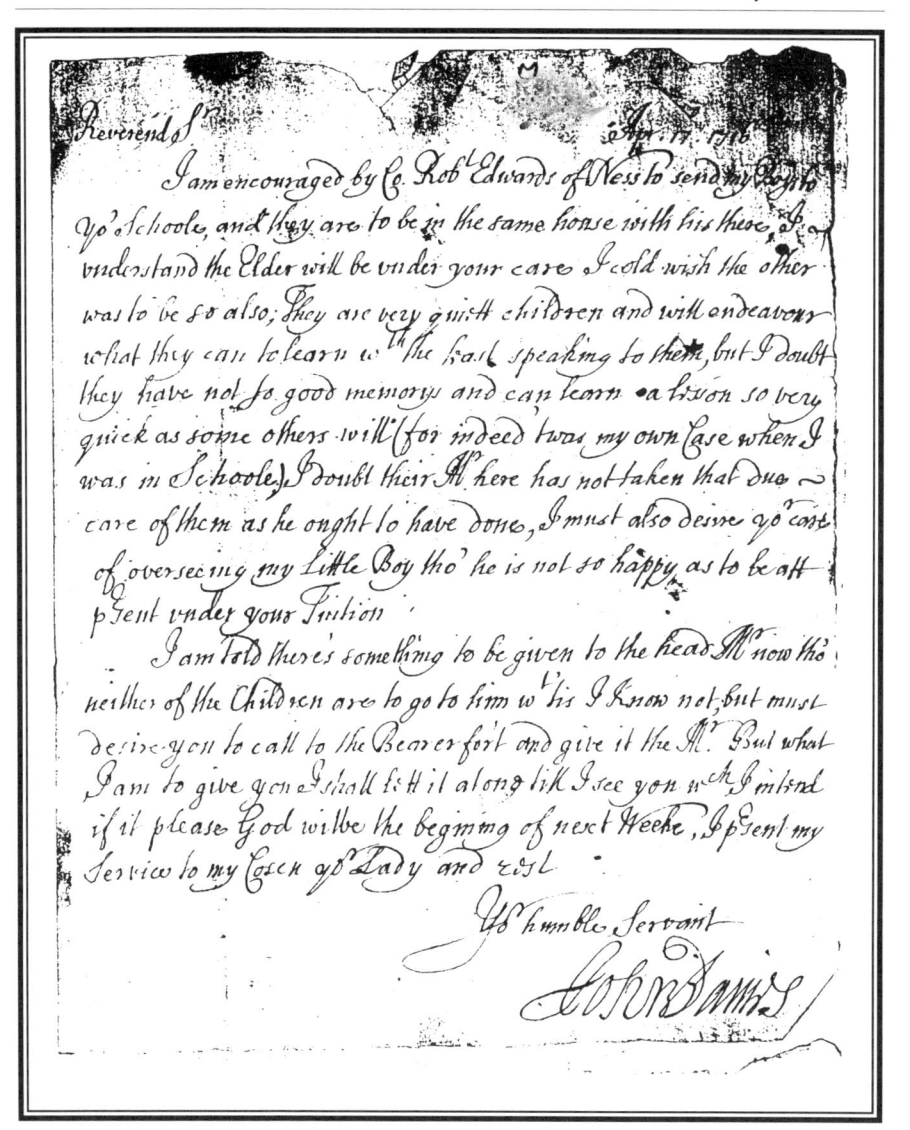

I am encouraged by Co. Robt Edwards of Ness to send my Boys to yor Schoole, and they are to be in the same house with his there. I vnderstand the Elder will be vnder your care I cold wish the other was to be so also; they are very quiett children and will endeavour what they can to learn wth the [last?] speaking to them, but I doubt they have not so good memorys and can learn a lesson so very quick as some others will (for indeed twas my own case when I was in Schoole) I doubt their Mr here has not taken that due care of them as he ought to have done, I must also desire yor care of overseeing my Little Boy tho' he is not so happy as to be att psent vnder your Tuition.

I am told there's something to be given to the head Mr now tho' neither of the Children are to go to him wth. 'tis I know not, but must desire you to call to the Bearer for't and give it the Mr. But what I am to give you I shall settle it along till I see you wch I intend if it please God wilbe the begining of next Weeke, I psent my Service to my Cosen yor Lady and rest

                                         Yor humble Servant
                                         John Davies

A letter from a parent to Samuel Garbet, dated April 17 1716.

These payments in nails are recorded amongst the cash payments which he listed for his scholars. Samuel also occasionally allowed some credit as some parents were often late settling their accounts. Many letters received from parents thank him for 'Taking care of their little boys', with anxious mothers requesting special attention for their offspring. One such request is amusing; John Rogers the guardian of Corbett Edwards, warns Samuel that:

> He is a child of wit and of consequence, of little conduct, he loves liberty... and he is a boy of spirit... and he will find an artful way of escape from Wem to Shrewsbury.'[124]

Others warn that their offspring are:

> very quiet children... and they do not have so good memories, and cannot learn a lesson, so very quick, as some others will.

In 1724 Peter Edwards resigned as the headmaster of Wem Free School.

> All the feofees came in a body and offered it to me, but I refused to accept their favour. The Rector pressed me to comply with their proposal, and Mr Tyler (the third master) wanted nothing more than me to move higher, that he might step into my place. But the ill state of my health, the badness of my voice, the difficulty in managing the 'Big Boys', the present emptiness of the head school, and the impossibility of filling it with such a second as I was like to have, determined me to adhere to my first resolution.[125]

Here is evidence of errors in the printed publication of 1818 which stated that Samuel had,

> ... refused to accept [the headship] in 1724, for several reasons, having for thirty years kept the credit of the school, and being in easy circumstances, he thought it fit to retire from that toilsome employment, and that at his leisure have the hours to complete these memoirs for the information of posterity.[126]

This last statement was almost certainly written in 1741 and not 1724: Samuel joined the school in 1711 and his thirty years would therefore have expired in 1741. In his diary he also stated that:

> Since 1734 Mr Appleton had but three scholars, but my school flourished continually. However, after near thirty years fatigue, I grew weary of it, and at Christmas did resign it.[127]

Samuel Garbet junior was taught by his father, yet one of the documents[128] indicates that he appears to have been placed in the lower school. On the 1 April 1734, Samuel proudly writes — 'My son set out for Oxford, and was admitted to Christchurch, upon the account that I was the first that gave the college notice of Carswell's charity'. Yet according to the *Victoria County*

History of Shropshire the first Carswell Scholarship* was not awarded until 1744.[129]

As Samuel settled to enjoy his retirement, and pursue his quest for local history, he and his son were almost part of an event in British history. A letter exists in the Garbet papers that reveals the consternation caused to both the Garbets and the townsfolk of Wem, by the nearness of the Jacobite army led by Charles Edward Stuart, as they marched from Warrington through Stone and thence to Derby. Rumours and counter rumours were flying between Chester, Nantwich and Shrewsbury and panic was rife in the area of Whitchurch and Wem.

On 6 December 1745 Samuel Garbet junior (then curate of Wem church) wrote to a Dr Penrose.

> God be thanked, we of this place have had a joyful deliverance after having been hurried three or four days successively with the most terrible apprehensions, and more than once thrown into confusion.

He then goes into detail how it was the design of the enemy to have marched directly from Wigan to Chester then on to Shrewsbury. He states that orders were given on 28 November

> ... to provide for the Duke at Namptwich [sic], who was at that time no further than Lichfield ... but these orders sent to all the Posthouses on the Chester road were sent to amuse.

He thought, however, that reports in the *London Evening Post* were misleading. He writes that:

> Ld Dby [Lord Derby?] withdrew the Lancashire militia and disbanded them, so 800 clever men immediately dispersed to their homes. This was imputed

---

* *Edward Carswell, Gentleman of Bobbington, Staffordshire, who, by his will dated 3 February 1689, devised that all his messuages, tenements and herediments, some 1,000 acres in total, within the counties of Staffordshire and Shropshire, then valued at between £400–£500 per annum, to certain trustees for the term of 500 years. This was for the maintenance of 18 scholars in Christchurch College, Oxford, allowing each of them the sum of £18-11s-0d over a period of four years, whilst they were undergraduates. This was to be increased to £21-11s-0d for a further three years after they had taken their batchelors degree and, after they had commenced their Master of Arts, the sum was again increased to £27-11s-0d for three years, but no longer. He proposed that four scholars from Shrewsbury School, three from Bridgnorth, four from Newport, three from Shifnal, two from Wem and two from Donnington, and with the rider that if the rents from his estates be increased and realise further income, additional scholars were to be sent to Christchurch [Victoria County History, Shropshire, Vol. 2, p.47].*[130]

to the want of officers; for country gentlemen who sometimes since were forward to accept commissions, were the first now to take care of themselves.

He next mentions a horseman who was dispatched from Wigan to Liverpool

... who rode up the town boldly, being well armed, to the Exchange where the mayor and Aldermen were assembled, to give the compliments of his Master the Duke of Perth who sent his excuses for passing by without a visit, as the Prince expected them to attend him at Chester. It appears the horseman was a local man who was put into irons for giving fright to the towns folk of Liverpool.

The entry into Manchester is described:

... all the bells ringing and all the bonfires lighted the whole town was illuminated.

It was then thought that the rebels were near Northwich and Middlewich 'this but 22 miles from us. the news of this made us that night very uneasy...' He records several false reports followed by true accounts of the armies at Stone and Leeke:

... at ten this morning a fellow came galloping thro' our town to read to some gentlemen in the street, particularly to some who had fled from Chester: a paper or express as he called it, that the Duke was on the road to Namptwhich [sic], from there to Whitchurch... this Varlet with his false intelligence threw Whitchurch into confusion. People were driving off their cattle, all the Chester strangers deserted the town and within one hour seven families, in as many coaches fled from one Inn ... Wednesday 4th The Duke marched southwards from Stone. Some gentlemen from our town, who were in Stone an hour after the army's departure ... for asking too many questions, were taken up for spies, but were released in the evening. They came home without daring to satisfy their curiosity any further ...'.

Just to make sure of his own safety, Samuel junior prepared his horse and put some shirts in his saddle bags 'intending to get twenty miles off at least'!

The Local Historian

Samuel Garbet had been collecting information on the history of Wem since he arrived in the town in 1713 and for the last decade of his life he wore a new hat, that of the local historian of Wem. There is no doubt that he knew his near neighbour Richard Gough of *The History of Myddle* fame. Gough had served as a clerk to Robert Corbett of Stanwardine Hall, and Samuel's sister-in-law Elizabeth Edwards was, prior to her marriage, a member of this family. Samuel's brother-in-law William Watkins of Shotton Hall in the parish of Myddle, one of the executors of the will of John Edwards of Great Ness (father-in-law to Samuel Garbet) was also well known, and mentioned many times by Gough in his *History of Myddle*, including this statement 'That this family was to become one of the most respected in the parish, both for their abilities and for their service to the community.'[131] This is a slightly different opinion to that held by Samuel Garbet, who spent near twenty years pressing the executors for a settlement of John Edwards' bequests.

Gough is described by Baily in *A Portrait of Shropshire* as 'The antiquarian of Myddle,' nothing exceptional in that. Gough drew on his sixty years of observations to produce the equivalent of today's gutter press gossip column, making a detailed exposure of the skeletons in the cupboards of all the families of the parish.[132] His description of Myddle is, however, much more than this. Hoskins, in the introduction to *The History of Myddle*, thought it may be the narrowest kind of parish pump history, but also a unique book for 'It gives a picture of 17th century England in all its wonderful and varied detail such as no other book that I know even remotely approaches'.[133] David Hay echoes Hoskins saying:

> It was a unique and remarkable book and one of the most valuable sources for the study of late Stuart England, that one could wish for.[134]

> This book includes a description of the parish itself, major monuments, lords of the manor and all the conventional subjects of local history married with all the local gossip, and most of it of a scandalous kind, being highly entertaining, which all adds up to a faithfull picture of his time.[135]

It has to be said that, by comparison, Garbet's *History of Wem* lacks the entertaining scandalous comments that appear in Gough's work. Yet in the printed copy of Volume IX of the *Wem Parish Registers*, the Reverend W. G. Fletcher states that:

> The history of this parish has been traced with some acuteness and considerable diligence by the Reverend Samuel Garbet, who preached at the Chapel of Edstaston in the parish of Wem for 43 years and was buried there 10th August 1756. Garbet, besides being a laborious, painstaking antiquary, lacked not humour, for he had a love of anecdotes, which, though not as scandalous as Gough's, are sufficiently refreshing. His printed work is unfortunately marred by serious typographical errors, and although every copy I have seen is dated 1818, internal evidence clearly indicates that the work was written circa 1740–1753.[136]

Garbet did not exhaust the store of information bearing on the history of

Wem, contained within the Episcopal Act Book of Lichfield. He did however make full use of the parish registers, a volume of which was missing when Fletcher first came to reside in the parish, but which he was fortunate to rediscover and 'restore it to its proper custody'.[137] Garbet may have also used a later volume of the church wardens' accounts for Wem 1684–1734, which was discovered in the 19th century, for his signature appears frequently in it from 1715 onwards.[138]

We have to pose the question — what prompted Samuel Garbet to undertake a town history? In the preface of *The History of Wem*, a book which which was intended to include the Hundred of North Bradford, Garbet states 'It has been long lamented that Shropshire has produced no author that has taken a survey of it, and published its natural and civil history, its antiquities and its present state.' He acknowledges

> That this county could indeed boast of famous Lawyer Plowden, the celebrated Hebrician Broughton and the learned divine, Dr Whichcote, the admirable linguists, Wheelock and Hyde [and] the excellent grammarians, critics and antiquaries Burton and Baxter. But, it still needs a Plot or an Ashmole to give a topographical and historical description of it. Mr Mytton lately undertook to supply this defect, and with that view has made very valuable collections; but the difficulties and discouragement he met with, prevented the execution of so good a design. Several years ago, I began my enquiries about Wem, which as time and opportunity serve, I shall carry through to North Bradford, but at present will confine myself to the allotments of Wem and Shawbury.'[139]

Garbet may have been influenced in his research by Mytton, whose original manuscripts are amongst the Garbet collection.

The format of the *History of Wem* is in fact similar to that of *The History of Myddle* which Hay sees as being 'In much the same vein as Camden'.[140] Gough describes the situation, the bounds of the parish, the church at Myddle and the chapel at Hadnell, patrons, rectors, clerks, fees and dues, then goes on to the lordship, owner of the manor, castle, park and warren, meres, commons, highways, manorial customs, and concludes with remarks on the involvement of the parish in the Civil War, and then wrote additionally of the families. Gough's descriptions of the lives of ordinary people during the 17th century is unsurpassed.[141]

Garbet, who incidentally was of a similar age to Gough, when he was writing his history, describes:

> The name of Wem, Boundaries, Extent of North Bradford, Natural History, Ecclesiastic and Civil divisions, The Parish Allotment and Civil Manor of Wem, The township and town of wem, The Barony and Barons of Wem,

Customs of the Jury, Bailiffs and Burgess's, Rectors, Curates, School masters. Dissenting Ministers, Wem during the Civil war, The Great Fire, Markets and Fairs, Streets, Lanes Common Fields and Charters.

The father of local history, we know as John Leyland, the clerical scholar who attracted royal favour. He introduced the idea of the 'Shire' as a unit for studying the history of Britain, and the idea took root. These ideas may have influenced Samuel, in proposing to include North Bradford Hundred in his history, and Dr Jenny Kermode, when writing in the *English County Histories*, states that 'town studies provide material often incorporated into later County Histories'.[142]

One's first impression of *The History of Wem*, is both the lack of illustrations and of the careful maps that Samuel made of the town, and which were a popular feature with publishers of that period. The lack of maps in the book is puzzling, for to the local historian they are a most important tool, whether drawn to scale by expert cartographers or are mere sketch maps of streets, fields and boundaries drawn by enthusiastic amateurs.

Within the Garbet papers are a number of important maps sketched by Samuel. These are of streets and burgage property allocations in Wem and also of varying outlying townships. Examination of one such map, that of the burgage plots and property in Wem, reveals in its detail the extent to which Samuel went in recording property ownership in the town. Hindle says 'That the very least maps should be viewed as a specific type of historical evidence, no better nor worse intrinsically than the written word or any other source'.[143] All maps are made for a particular purpose, but both maps and documents can be misleading if not understood and interpreted correctly.

Garbet's maps were drawn between 1720 and 1750 and, although not to scale, present a reasonably accurate picture and depict his interest in the town burgage plots and the ownership of property in Wem during the 17th and 18th centuries. It has been a very difficult exercise trying to locate the site of his home and his other burgage plots in New Street, despite a search of all the deeds of New Street held in the Shropshire Record Office. A comparison of Garbet's map with the plan of Wem dated 1834 shows that the outline of the original burgage plots is almost identical with the boundaries outlined in the later map.[144]

The tithe map is of too late a date to give accurate information on Wem in the early 18th century but the title deeds to various properties in New Street inform us that one Samuel Walmsly of Creamore had property in New Street which was occupied in about 1834, by the Rev Walter Gough, and

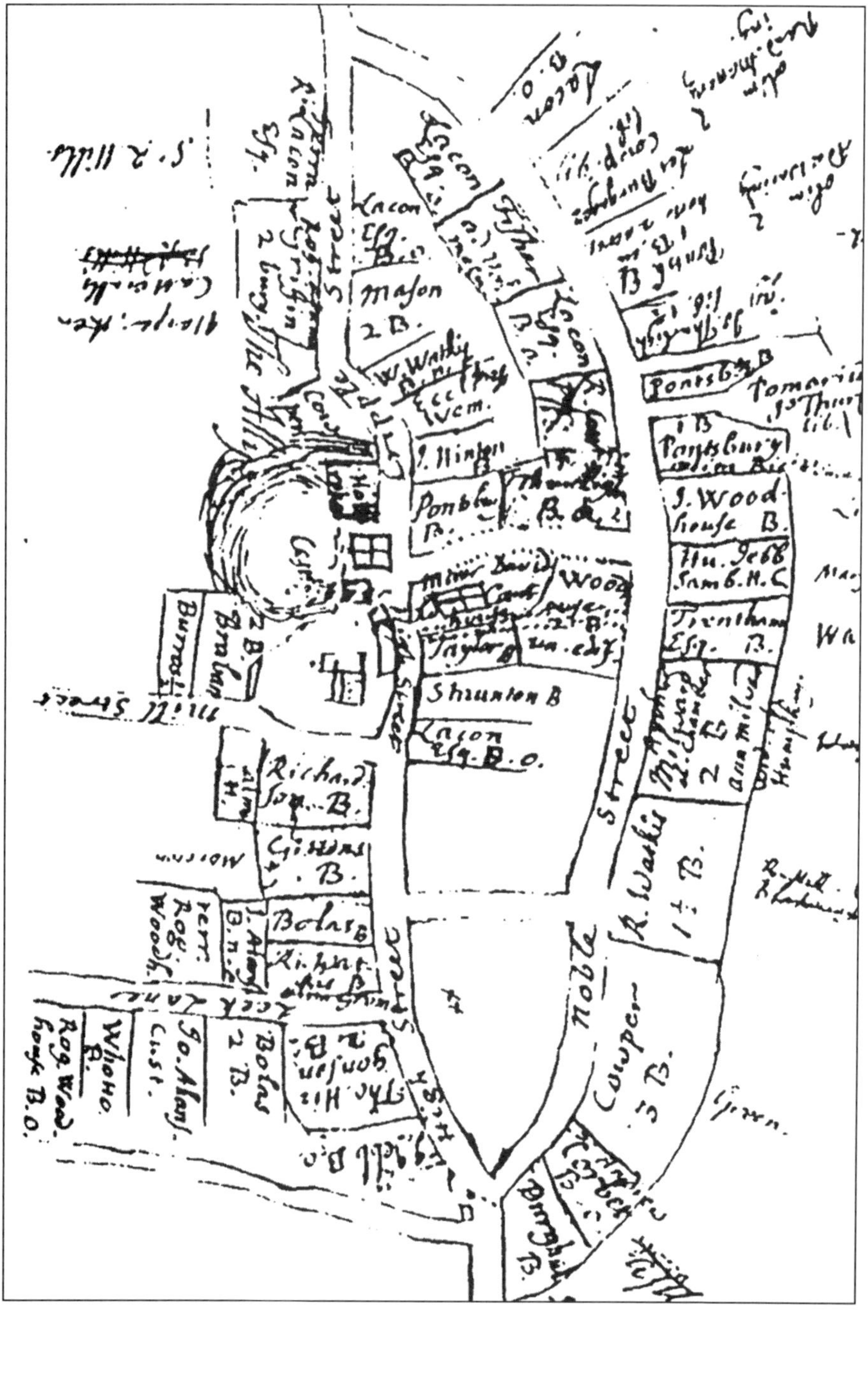
Noble Street
Mill Street
Mason 2 B.
J. Woodhouse B.
Lacon Esq. B.O.
Cowper 3 B.
Green

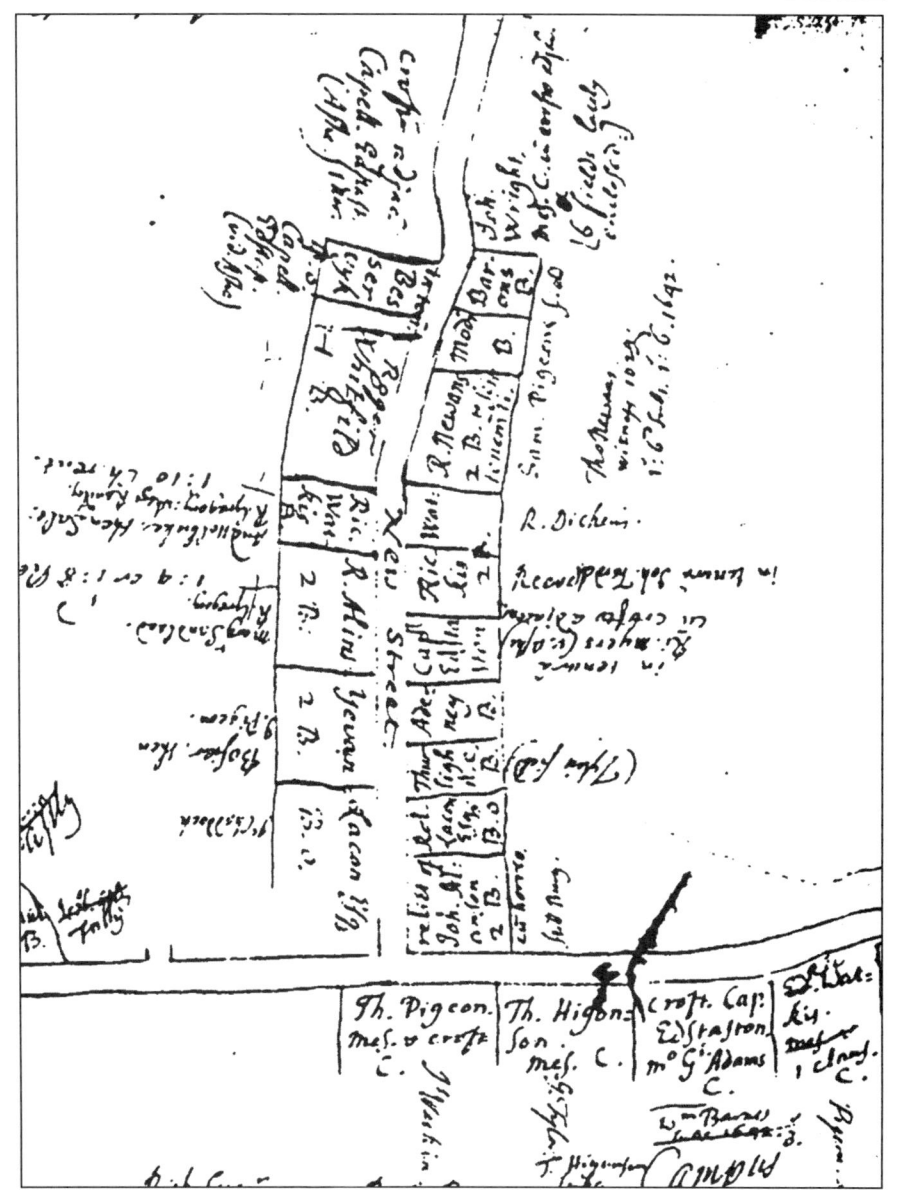

Facing: Sam Garbet's map of Wem: the section showing Cripple Street, Noble Street, Leek Street and Mill Street.

Above: Sam Garbet's map of Wem: the section showing New Street.

previously occupied by a Mr John Hawksworth, and before that by the Rev Thomas Sandiland (who was a tenant of Samuel Garbet junior in c1760. Walter Gough is clearly listed on the 1834 town map of Wem,[145] almost on the same site as the burgage bought from the Wingfield family by Sam senior in 1715. But Samuel Garbet owned four burgage plots in New Street, so the location of his home is still unknown although the jig-saw of his other properties in Wem is being completed.

Throughout his book, he attempts not to be scandalous, but does acknowledge his sources, not in the scholarly manner which would be acceptable today, but by odd comments made here and there e.g. 'Mr Richard Allanson, Bailiff of the Manor, to whose candour and humanity I owe several lights, that have enabled me to traverse the dark paths of antiquity.' It would appear that Richard Allanson gave Garbet access to the Manorial Court Rolls and other documents. He also mentions Mr Mytton in his preface, and there is a two page document with Mr Mytton's account of Wem, taken from Lloyd's manuscripts, entitled 'Wem Market Town'.

At a meeting of The Archaeological Institute of Hereford in 1877, the speaker, Mr C. J. Robinson, said:

> That to be a good historian of a County, a man should possess a variety of qualifications; Vigourous Health, Studious Habits, Untiring Patience, and a Facile pen should be his; but above all he should have a full purse and a vein of stubborn but unobtrusive scepticism.

Samuel Garbet qualified in all the above requirements with the exception of the first, that of vigourous health. The first comments on his health are reported in 1723, when the chapel at Edstaston was being rebuilt. He records that he

> ... contracted a great disorder which not only impaired my health, but much obstructed my voice, no one had been used to speak with more ease than I, but now I could seldom speak without difficulty and frequently without straining.

Again in 1724, his health was one of the reasons he declined the headship of Wem School; 'The ill state of my health and the weakness of my voice.'[146] On 30 September 30 1729, he states:

> I myself fell into a disorder, that hung on me for four months. It was a fever of the spirits, which entirely deprived me of sleep. 2nd of November I was so bad, that I sent for Dr Wingfield, who recommended a more generous diet than that Mr Astley had allowed me.[147]

There is nothing more until 1744:

My health which had been very bad at the end of 1736 and which some thought that I should entirely lose. But upon giving up the school [1741] it did sensibly improve and grow better.[148]

On 15 August 1754, exactly two years before he died, his resignation was considered by the Reverend Sam Smallbroke, who said 'Sir, resignations when so voluntary as yours, are such unusual things that I cannot help desiring you to reconsider. As your health has been impaired and you complain of so much additional weakness.'[149]

The pursuit of local history all too often proved to be the ruin of health and wealth.* The founding father himself, John Leyland, went mad.[150] Whether or not the pursuit of local history did play a part in Samuel's ill health, we may never know, but his personal papers reveal that it had become an obsession. He produced not only town maps, but also maps of most of the townships. From jottings made on many scraps of paper, we find he recorded the history of prominent land owning families, together with those of yeomen and ordinary townsfolk.

He appears to have been a friend of William Mytton (1693–1746), a younger son of the Halston family, who was neighbour of Edward Lloyd (1660–1709) of Loppington, a man described by G. C. Baugh as 'The Polymoth, who would be difficult to overlook.'[151] By 1731, Mytton designed towards a County History and between 1732 and 1736 he journeyed around Shropshire with a young assistant, James Bowen, inspecting registers and title deeds, but eventually died in Hubberley in 1746, having published nothing.

Samuel's friendship with Mytton, and the fact that he had purchased a number of county histories, together with letters requesting information on historical topics, reveal a deep personal interest not only in the history of the locality wherein he now resided, but also of an intention to publish his findings. He was now in a period of his life when he could enjoy the income from his various properties and had the leisure time to do so, bearing in mind he had already published and sold two translations of *The Book of Phaedrus*.

In 1750, Samuel started to compile an account of the family's history, containing details of his predecessors and information concerning his own life. Unfortunately, this, together with other papers in the collection, have been mutilated by someone cutting and snipping certain sections out. It is also disappointing in that as Houlbrook points out, 'Nearly all diarists

---

* Samuel Garbet junior was also noted for problems with his health: 'Nov 5 bad health for a week, ... Jan 30 1737 ill health till Easter', and eventually in 1747 resigned as Curate of Wem Church, because his weak constitution could not cope with the demands of the job.

remain silent about certain areas of their lives; but that these areas varied from one diarist to the next.'[152]

Samuel certainly remains silent on many aspects of his life, which have to be gleaned from other sources. His sense of humour is dry and on occasions caustic, but he was always fair in his assessment of contemporaries, even those, it would appear, whom he did not like or approve of. He always stressed their good points and was almost unbiased in giving an opinion. In the fly-leaf of the Edstaston Chapel Register of March 1727 he states 'That this book was bought at his own expense for use at Edstaston Chapel, Wem Parish, by Mr Daniel Payne, father of Thomas Payne, the last of that foolish race'.[153]

Of Henry, Lord Newport, he describes his visit to Wem during the reign of Queen Anne, with the final comment:

> That he died of Gout on 27th December 1734, and was buried in the abbey church at Westminster. His body was handsome and well made, of moderate stature, inclinable to be fat. He had good natural parts, was affable, generous, kind and obliging. Amongst a great many good qualities he had one imperfection, that he chose to keep Captain Smith's wife rather than marry a wife of his own![154]

Of Andrew Parsons, a rector of Wem who died in 1684, he says 'He was a devout and religious man, a laborious and pathetic preacher',[155] and of Reese Hughes, 'He could never speak English like a native; was a mean preacher of the gospel,and a worse economist of secular affairs, which involved him in troubles and an occasional spell in gaol'.[156] Hughes had died in 1670 so where did Samuel obtain such information? Robert Eyton, rector from 1718–51 is described thus:

> He was a tall handsome personal man. His voice was strong, distinct and agreeable. His deportment in Divine Service was not always grave and serious, but no one could behave better when he was so disposed. he had a very good natural parts, but was indolent to take pains to cultivate them by reading and study.[157]

Samuel was not very well disposed to Robert Eyton, rector of Wem, for when Eyton ordered Samuel to read prayers in Wem church every third week he said: 'This was a great imposition, yet for peacesake it was complied with for many years'.[158] Stephen Prytherch, headmaster of Wem School in 1748, was described by Samuel 'As a Cambro-Briton, he is an agreeable and well accomplished man, reads distinctly, sings admirably and so is an agreeable companion as well as a good scholar.'[159] This is the nearest we will discover of Samuel's closest friends.

The Reverend John Collier, Samuel's predecessor at Estaston Chapel ...
Was of middle stature, a sanguine complexion, his face flamed by drink. He was not eminent as a scholar or divine, but was a well respected a sportsman, and a good companion. He was always busy at election times and therefore got the presentation of Great Ness.

This of course was the living that Samuel was very much hoping for.[160] Of Francis Allanson, son of William Allanson of New Street, Wem, — 'Married a lewd and extravagant virago from London, who by her riotous and expensive living ran him far into debt, that he had to sell his estate.'[161]

Samuel obviously enjoyed humour for he notes that in 1640, 'That the eldest son of Daniel Whycherly was born near Wem! Who proved to be one of the greatest wits and most eminent comic poet that England had produced.'[162] Of Lord Jefferys, son of George Jeffreys, the Lord Chancellor, 'he was a little man, rakish, like a debauchee of quality, he affected wit and versified by way of frolic.'[163]

Samuel continued to write his history almost to the end, Samuel Garbet junior, informs us of those last days of his father's life 'That in 1754, Mr Samuel Garbet senior, laboured during the greater part of August under a dangerous boil in the shoulder, who's sinuses spread very far over his back.'[164] 'The winter proved mild, until the month of March, then the north east winds set in, severely cold. Mr Garbet, who would not be diverted from his wanted amusement in his beloved garden, had the first attack of the palsy.'[165] On 19 March he had a severe stroke, and another three days later, which affected the lower limbs, and also the left side, and a stiffness in the cheek, and his limbs began to swell. Mr Whitefield of Shrewsbury attended him that day, and 'bled him plentifully'. A course of medicine gave him the desired relief and he was

> ... prudently restrained to the house till the return of warm weather in June. For some weeks after he first went abroad he complained of his left cheek, being cold in the daytime and burning at night But even this relict of the disorder was almost quite worn off. His good spirits and complexion were recovered and the strength of his hand in great measure restored, only with fainter sensation than is natural, yet he was attacked yet again and the added discomfort of water retention... His Apothacary thought proper to administer a clyster which worked as a purgative too strongly but excited no urine.

Again he was blooded. By now the advice of a surgeon was required and Mr Blakeway of Shrewsbury attended, who thought he felt a stone in the bladder. Samuel was by now suffering from an enlarged prostrate and an infected urethra, due probably to the misuse of a catheter and would have been in great pain.[166] By Friday 30 March the attendance of a more eminent surgeon was obtained, and a Mr Price came and advised 'sitting in a warm bath', but to no effect. By now Samuel had 'a strong apprehension of his danger' and gave orders to his son about the disposal of certain papers and directed him to give £80 to his old servant Mary Hinton. He often prayed that God would receive his soul.

On Thursday 5 August, early in the morning, he gave his benediction to his son and the following day surrendered to him the keys to his study and scritoire. On Saturday, at six in the morning, he was

> ... seized with a strong shivering, his left arm was motionless, his eyes became fixed and the agony continued till past noon. About two o'clock he departed with much ease at the age of 71 years and upwards of 6 months. [167]

Conclusion
He passed away quietly on an August day in 1756, no doubt with as much dignity as he could muster, after so painful an illness. So, after his demise, what conclusions can be drawn form this study of the Reverend Samuel Garbet?

His background is from the 'Petty Gentry' or gentleman farming stock. He had always been accustomed to a comfortable home, with servants and, more importantly to Samuel, a 'Good Table'. Though he lived in an age when education was taken lightly, he appears to have been studious, and thus continued to improve his mind throughout his life.

With his father and grandfather so influenced by church life, Samuel through his writing portrays a serious, but not grave disposition. On the other side of the coin, his attitudes are gentle, displayed by his payment of money to children, his tenderness towards Martha Wingfield and the few but loving comments about his dear Anna, his partner for fifteen years, whom he described as 'one of the best of women, handsome, genteel, well bred'. Though one may question the haste of this union, it proved to be a strong and loving partnership.

His social conscience is also evident in other aspects of his life: as curate of Edstaston Chapel, where he served for 43 years, organising payments to the poor, the purchase of the chalice and even to the painting of the pulpit at his own expense. He also procured bread for the poor of Edstaston to be given for three weeks of each month. Mr Daniel Payne gave on the fourth week. As a schoolmaster and translator, the letters from parents are quite clear as to their opinion of his abilities as a teacher. Their appreciation of his loving care of those pupils who lodged with him, and of his refusal to deny anyone an education, by taking payment in kind.

He was a cultivated and widely read man who believed in a good appearance. His clothes may not have been stylish, but he was certainly well turned out in good, serviceable wear. He was a lively and witty conversationalist, who did not suffer fools gladly, as many of his caustic comments bear witness.

He married into one of the great border families, the Edwards' of Great Ness and Lledrud, and although causing upsets by his many enquiries into the wills of both John and Dorothy Edwards, he was respected by the family, and it was due to his efforts as a mediator, that the 'Virginia Affair' was brought to an acceptable conclusion.

He knew the value of owning both property and land, and its implication with regard to his standing within local society. He was an understanding and careful landlord, never hesitating to spend money on repairs to his property. Sadly, we find within this study, that he made several applications for other livings, and despite good references, was never successful. This was because he lacked patronage, and as he was too independent a man to be in anyone's pocket, he would never have dreamt of soliciting votes at election times to gain patronage, and thus remained as curate at Edstaston for all those years.

He entertained, was a well accepted member of Wem society, and enjoyed good company. He was well respected by local tradesmen as he was known to always pay his bills in full, as he did with all his local taxes.

Unfortunately his health was always suspect, and he did suffer from periods of depression, some serious, although he always improved from them. His sole passions in life, were his beloved garden and his pursuit of local history. He was fortunate in his friendship with William Mytton, and in all probability knew Richard Gough.

As a local historian, he acknowledged all his sources, a most unusual trait in his day, and his cartographic skills and maps will prove to be of immense value to future historians of Shropshire. This learned man left his mark in Wem, where he was regarded as careful and astute and was known throughout the district as the 'Goode Mr Garbet'.

If he had one weakness, it was his love for his son, Samuel junior and was blind to his many faults —or was he simply turning a blind eye to protect him from scandalous accusations? A week before his death, 'having strong apprehension of his danger', he gave orders to his son about the disposal of certain papers; and on thursday 5 August he gave his benediction to Samuel, before departing this life two days later. It seems strange, however, that two

Samuel Garbet's grave (foreground) at Edstaston Church, near Wem.

men of the cloth, together in a sick room and knowing that the hour of departure was near, failed to make any provision for a will and testament. As a result, Samuel Garbet junior declared that his father had died intestate — one occasion when we may question the integrity of Samuel junior.

Another similar occasion was when James Garbet died in 1739, leaving his estate to his nephew Samuel Garbet junior. His father received two very pointed letters from the vicar of St Alkmund's of Shrewsbury, with regard to Samuel junior's refusal to honour a bequest from his uncle, in that he was to pay the poor of that parish an annual sum from James Garbet's estate. The vicar claimed 'That you sir are the person in whose integrity your brother absolutely confided, as to leave the affair entirely in your son's hands, who he doubted not, would inherit your good qualities, as well as be under your influence.' Would that the son had the same qualities of his late lamented father.

Although Samuel Garbet senior was, by profession, a cleric and school master, it was his passion for local history that enabled him to be recognized as the first historian of Wem and as one of the earliest local historians in Shropshire, and it is for his work in this field that he is now remembered.

After his death on 7 August 1756, Samuel Garbet's body was taken to Edstaston Chapel which he had served for 43 years, for burial on 10 August beside his wife, in the chapel yard. The following epitaph (translated from the Latin*), composed by his son and inscribed on the tombstone is a fitting conclusion to this dissertation.

NEAR TO THE REMAINS OF HIS EXCELLENT WIFE
DID HE WISH TO BE LAID
SAMUEL GARBET A.M.
FITTING TEACHER IN THE RUDIMENTS OF HUMANITY
WITH WHICH HE IMBUED MANY,
TO OUTSTANDING TEACHING IN THIS HOUSE
DEVOTED HIMSELF FOR 43 YEARS.
CARRYING OUT THOSE DUTIES WITH PRAISE,
HE WILLINGLY ESCHEWED ANYTHING MORE.
HE WAS A MAN OBSERVING MODERATION IN EVERY
WAY OF LIFE,
UPRIGHT WITHOUT DECEIT,
AND EAGER FOR PEACE AND VIRTUE ALIKE.
VERSED IN THE LEARNING OF A MORE GRACEFUL TIME,
IN HIS OLD AGE HE DEVOTED HIS WORK TO ANTIQUITY
AND EXPLAINED THE HISTORY OF THE TOWN.
TO UNAVOIDABLE ILLNESS
IN TRANQUILLITY JUST AS HE HAD LIVED
HE YIELDED AD 1756 AGED 73.
S.G. jnr.

* *Translated in 1995 by Jaquie Crosby, Lancashire Record Office.*

64 *The Goode Mr Garbet of Wem*

Appendix I
The Church Lewn for Wem.

Quarter ffor ye year 1731 att 2s1/2 p pound. Francis Sandland church warden.

High Street	£	s	d
The Earl of Bradford for shop & ware land		2	11
Andrew Corbett Esq for wrights		1	0^1/2
Mr Jno Jebb or tent^t		1	3
Peter Pidgion			3^3/4
Mr Montgomery or tent part void			5
Widw Pidgeon			7^1/2
Thoms Pidgeon			10
George Car			7^1/2
Edward Jones			7^1/2
Robert Sandland or tent^t		3	6^1/2
Mr Walford		2	1
Mr Wood		4	9^1/2
Char Booth 5d and for Lady Meadows		2	1
Tho Griffiths		1	0^1/2
Mr Tho Whitfield or tent for ye ward		4	7^1/2
Joseph Pixley			3^3/4
Mr Cooper or tent^t		9	2
Arther Jones for widw Davies			5
James Chaddock			3^3/4
Jno Swannick		1	0^1/2
Richard Tyler for Sayers		1	5^1/2
Jno Fardoe ffor Rowleys		1	3
Tim Parker or tent Watts		2	1
And ffor Rounile		1	5^1/2
Mr Tho Whitfield for his Houses		1	6^3/4
The worshipfule ye Rev Mr Eyton for ye land			
Pidgeons & Ashford		3	5^3/4
Mr Green for Evans voyd or poore		0	0
Ralp Wells for Russells			5
Richard Hughes or tent^t		3	5^1/2
Mr Fox for Houses & Land		3	10^1/2
Joseph Lee		1	3
Mr Jones			11^1/4
Tho Higginson or Mr Tiler			2^1/2
Mr John Dickin		1	5^1/2
Mos Parker		1	5^1/2

The Goode Mr Garbet of Wem 65

Mr Wm Shent or tent[t]	1	3
Anne Amies		3³/₄
Mr Wilson	2	1
Mr Kilburn ffor part		10
Mr Richard Tyler ffor part		7¹/₂
Jno Davies	1	3
Mr Wilson ffor manloves shop		5
Isaac Gregory		10
Wid Dean	2	9³/₄
Jne Ebrey ffor part or tent[t]		8³/₄
Wid Forgham ffor Mr Shenton	8	9
Mr Wickstead	2	1
Thos Higginson or tent[t]		7¹/₂
Mr Goldsberg	1	0¹/₂
Samuel Barnes	1	5¹/₂
Mr Wickstead ffor Salts		9¹/₂
Mr Atcherly for M[s] Adams	5	7¹/₂
Bennets Shop		5
Mr Astley	3	9
Mr Higgins	1	5¹/₂
Mr Taylor		10
Dovenport or tent[t]	1	0¹/₂
Mr Guest	1	3
Robert Sandland	1	5¹/₂
Wm Allinson		7¹/₂
Richard Allinson		7¹/₂
Jno Smith		7¹/₂
Mr Richardson or tent[t]		5
Wid Griffiths ffor part		5
Mr James Lowe		8³/₄
Jn Barks		5
Richard Philips part void		4
Benj Blakemor		10
Wid Salmon		6¹/₂
Mr Tyler or tent for Basnett	1	5¹/₂
Richard Herrington or widw ffor Basnet	2	7³/₄
Jn Randles or tent[t] James Forgham		6¹/₄
Sr Row Hill or tent[t] Wickstead	2	5
Sam Shenton	1	3
Mr Higginson or tent[t]	1	8
Mary Pugh		5

66   The Goode Mr Garbet of Wem

Horse Yard

Mr Moody or tent void part		5
Mr Wickstead ffor Jno Williams ???	1	5¹/₂
Jno Burton or tent^t		7¹/₂
Mr — or tent^t	5	6
Mr Barnes or tent^t		11¹/₄
Henry Parton ffor ???	8	9
Mr Wicksteed ffor Tarver ???	1	0¹/₂
Earl of Bradford or tent^t ffor Ffridays	1	3
Jn ??? Kynaston or tent^t		5

Noble Street

Randle Cooke or tent^t		5
Tho Heath or tent^t now Mr Wicksteed voyd		0
Edward Williams or tent^t		5
Mr Bayley or tent^t		2¹/₂
Thos Owen		3³/₄
Mr Leigh or tent^t		10
Jno Sandland	1	3
Jno Deakin or tent^t		8³/₄
Mr Wilson ffor woodhouse	1	5¹/₂
Mr Lowe or tent^t for part		6
Mr Merygold		5
Wm Wycherly Esq		10
Robert Blakey	2	7³/₄
Mary Bennions Hous Wid Dean		2¹/₂
Widw Sherret ffor Mr Green	14	4¹/₂
Peter Pidgeon ffor a piece towards as[t]on		6¹/₂
Mr Green or tent^t ffor barnes prees ???		5
Edward Barnes		7¹/₂
Mr Astley ffor part of Mr Jebbs		10¹/₂
Mr Barnes		3¹/₂
Hodnett P^sh or tent^t ffor part	1	9¹/₄
Tho Griffiths		5

New Street

Mr Goldsbrough	2	6
Jno Pidgeon ffor Halls pese [piece]	5	2¹/₂
Jno Fox or tent^t		3³/₄
Wm Price		7¹/₂
The Rev Mr Garbet		11¹/₄
Mr Larrence	2	6

Jonathan Pool ffor pt of Mr Sandland void   0 0
Robert Walford   5
Mr Higginson ffor Hughes $7^1/4$
Broghalls Pitt   5

Cripple St
Mr Hesketh or tent^t 1 $0^1/2$
Andrew Allinson $7^1/2$
Jno Thomas $7^1/2$
Mr Rich Cooper ffor houses & lands   1 $10^1/2$
Mr Arther Wykey   10
Sam Wilkinson or tent^t part voyd $1^1/4$
Edward Jones   5
Jno Phillips   5
Tho Price $7^1/2$
Jas Lees   5
Jno Hails $7^1/2$
Wm Thomas $7^1/2$
Dr Whitfield & Mr Wood ffor part $8^3/4$
Mr Wicksteed ffor part $8^3/4$
The Rev Mr Garbett ffor part   1 $4^1/2$
Mr Tho W[h]itfield ffor part $5^1/2$
Wid Forgham   4 2

Mill Street
Frances Sandland ???   5
Jams Philips   1 $0^1/2$
Ed Humpkerson ffor House & lees void ???   0 0
Joseph Ashford $8^3/4$
Jhn Peckett [Beckett?] $7^1/2$
Wid Maddox $3^3/4$
Mr Jeffreys ffor ye Mills   6 3
Mr Barnet ffor Lambs Land ???   2 11
Mr Hughes or tent^t Barnes   4 7

Pool Land
Mr Chetloes assines ffor Dolman ???   6 3
Mr Wilson ffor Abnett   11 $7^1/2$
Mr Tyler or tent^t Evans Rd of Fferrington ??? 1 3
Mr Wikstead ffor Robins   10
Sr Rowland Hill or tent^t Mr Wicksteed   2 $4^3/4$
Mr Loveskin or tent^t 2 11

Mr Hughes or tentᵗ	1	8
Jno Barnes Esq or tentᵗ part	3	6¹/2
Bur Wingfield Esq or tentᵗ part	6	3
Mr Colley	1	10
Mr Atcherly or tentᵗ	1	0¹/2
Mr Chettoes Assign or tentᵗ Hales	6	3
Mr Wilson —	2	11
Mrs Denstone or tentᵗ	3	6¹/2
Sr Row Hill or tentᵗ Brown		7¹/2
Wm Puliston		5
Thoms Dean ffor Reynolds void		0

Appendix II
Register of Pupils of Wem Grammar School, 1719–37
NB the symbol • is believed to represent 'died'.

Fr's head class 1719
- Dan: Payne
- Rich Manlove from Loppington
- Roger Trevor   • eldest son of Sir Roger Trevor of Bodynvel
- Thos Trevor   Vic'r of Oswestry
- John Pryce   10/s
- John Chetto

His Head class 1720
- John Howard
- Rich. Davies   (son of ... of Trewylen)
- Bennet Dorset
- Thos. Vaughan of Cy Wood   •
- Sam Barnes   Clerks son
- Tho. Payne   of Noneley

His head class 1721
- Franc. Astly
- Rich. Lawrence   Vicar of ... Kent
- Gee Tyler   Pepper Street
- James Lowe   Isaac Chaddock was sent away 1720
- Edw. Best

Head class 1722
- Rich. Pigeon
- Thos. Tyler   5/s
- Joseph Swanwick
- Benj. Wingfield   (Minister of St. Mary's Salop)
- Robt. Davies   3/s   •   1748 of Tilley
- Thos. Pulistern 2/6d

Sam. Barnes
Mr Thomas Barnes went away 1721

The Second School

1st Class 1723
- Tho. Payne   Edstast. •
- Francis Finch
- John Lawrence 5/s   Chas Bowdler went away 1722
                         Rich. Phillips went away 1721
- Rich. Groom   Grocer. 1724 put back to lower class

2nd Class
- Roger Acherley

Loyd Edwards
William Higgins
Joh Whitfield   Surgeon
Tho. Whitfield of the Ware put in lower class 1725
Tho: Humphreyson   1724 in the lower class

3rd Class
Rich. Sandiland   Butcher
Thos. Chetto   (Mercer at Oxon)
John Chambre 10/6d gone 1724

Tho. Higgins
John Richards 2/6d   gone 1724
Sam. Sandiland
Tho. Harris   gone 1724
John Tyler   Pepper St.
John Davies   at Y Crown (1746)
Robt. Hassal   gone 172
Jim Parker   gone 172
Isaac Gregory
Bernard Dean gone 172
John Forgham gone 172

[The following name written upside down at the bottom of the page: Rich. Slater Moreton]

4th Class
Sam. Garbet   [Samuel Garbet's son]
Edw. Trevor   • Filo de se 1746
John PArker
Tho. Heath   gone 1724
Tho. Chidley   gone 1724
Sam. Pigeon
Robt. Bellingham   gone 1724
John Gregory   gone 1724   Barber
Lawr. Higginson
Sam. Phillips   gone 1726
Rich. Eaton   gone 1726
Thos. Gregory Here 1726   Parson

1724 Lower Class
Thos. Hayward   •
John Barnes   Seaman 1747
Tho. Dean
Tho. Gollins   gone 1725
John Hassal   gone 1727
Bold Burton

Wm. Forgham gone 1726
Tho. Meredith here 1727

1725 Lowest Class
John Randals   gone 1728
Mich. Mason   2/6d gone 1727
Rich. Astley
Rich. Cooper
Joseph Higginson   gone 1728
Francis Sandiland   here in 1726
Thos. Leak   on this bench gone 1728
John Salusbury here in 1726

1726 Lowest Class
John Appleyard   5/s Gone 1727
John Embrey   Gone 1728
John Wicksteed
Thos. Bury   Gone 1727   •
John Whitfield
Henry Wood   here in 1727 gone next year

1727 Lowest Class
Rich Harper   5/s   Tanners son
Rich. Price   •
Will. Shore
Rich. Frogham 26d   here in 1728

1728 Lowest Class
John Hand
Fred. Shenton   Gone before 1731

1729 Lowest Class
John Colley   Gone before 1731
Phil. Holland
Tho. Griffiths
Wm. Woodhouse   Gone before 1731

Next Class   John Bellingham
Here before 1731   John Groom   Gone 1733
Wm. Hayward into ye guards
here before 1732   Robt. Adams   Gone 1733 soldier

Next Class which was ye 3rd 1732
Steph. Steventon   Gone 1734
Rich. Chambre
Wm. Basnet

Tho. Walford
Tho. Dicken 7/6d
Wm. Embrey Gone 1733 • 1748
Wm. Eddowes
Wm. Fox

Next Class which was 1733
John Tiler of Coton 1733 I was bearer
Franc Chambre
Arthur Dicken Seaman
Robt. Morgan
Andr. Barnes Soldier Gone 1734
Robt. Embrey
Geo. Tiler • at London
Wm. Whitfield
Robt. Blackburn Here 1734
Arthur Beardmore Here 1734

Next class which was 3rd 1734
Thos. Eddowes
John Appleton
Tho. Leigh
John Holland
Rich. Sandland
Richard Bellingham
Sam. Jones
Thos. Acherley
John Astley
Baduley Townshend Here 1735

Next Class
Edw. Jones
Cornel Whitfield
Edw. Hand put lower before 1735
Edw. Morgan
 and afterwards in this class
Wm. Lawrence
James Prachet
Tho. Prachet

Head Class 1718
Geo. Wyke 10/6d
And. Mucklestone 5/0d
Rich. Hatchet 5/0d
Edw. Barret 2/6d

Head Class 1717
   Rich. Scriven   5/0d
   John Barnes   10/0d Lowe
   Chas. Harding 10/9d

Head Class 1716
   John Lacon   10/9d   son of the steward of the Manor
   Corbet Edwards   •
   Thos. Barret   10/0d
   Vaughan Barret   2/6d
   Edmund Pryce 10/9d
   Robt. Cleaton
   Robt. Binnell   2/6d

1715
   Robt. Edwards
   Edw. Cleaton
   Edw. Lyth   5/0d heir of the Estate at Walcot
   Benjm. Muclestone
   Joseph Garlean 5/0d

1714
   Will. Somerfield
   Will. Holbrook 5/0d
   John Dykes   5/0d

1713
   Sturdy   2/6d
   Young   2/6d

   Holbrook left school 1713

Notes

1. After lying for many years in solicitors' files in Wrexham, the same firm that was established by Samuel Garbet's grandson.
2. SGP/Y13.
3. SGP/Y13.
4. SGP/Y13.
5. *Fairburns General Armory*. Arms of the Garbet family. Gules, a griffon segreant or, supporting a knight's banner argent, flowing to the sinister, and there upon displayed a double-headed eagle, sable. Crest: Mantled and upon a wreath an imperial eagle as on the banner. Motto: *Gare Le Bete*. On a red shield a gold griffon, wings outspread, back to back, supporting a knights banner, on which is displayed a black double-headed eagle. Crest: Upon a wreath and mantle, a black double-headed imperial eagle as displayed on the knight's banner. Motto: 'Beware of the Beast', a play on the name Garbet. Granted by King Henry VII to Robert Garbet, Yeoman of the Guard.
6. SGP/Y13.
7. SGP/ Y13.
8. Ibid.
9. Ibid.
10. Webb S. &B., *The Parish and the County 1906–1963*, p.489.
11. SGP/Y13.
12. SGP/Y13.
13. Ibid.
14. Garbet Samuel, *The History of Wem*, 1818, p.200.
15. SGP/ Y13.
16. SGP/Y13.
17. SGP/Y13.
18. Ibid.
19. Ibid.
20. Christchurch College archives.
21. SGP/Y13.
22. Ibid.
23 Ibid.
24. SGP/Y13.
25. Ibid.
26. Ibid.
27. Ibid.
28. SGP/Y13.
29. Ibid.
30. S. Garbet, *The History of Wem*, 1818, p.208.
31. SGP/Y13.

32. Ibid.
33. SGP/Y13.
34. Ibid.
35. Ibid.
36. Ibid.
37. Ibid.
38. S. Garbet *History of Wem*, 1818, p.202.
39. *Armorial Bearings & Shropshire Families*, MS 4082, S.R.O.
40. SGP/Y13.
41. Ibid.
42. Ibid.
43. Ibid.
44. Will of Francis Garbet, Wroxeter, 1661, Lichfield. ROB/C11.
45. Ibid.
46. Will of Samuel Garbet of Norton, 1710. LRO.B/C/11.
47. Will of Thomas Garbet Norton, 1723. LRO. B/C/11.
48. Will of Francis Garbet of Walcot, 1737. LRO. B/C/11.
49. SGP/Y13.
50. SGP/B43a.
51. SGP/B76.
52. Ibid.
53. Garbet Wills, LRO.
54. SGP/B33.
55. SGP/B35.
56. SGP/B34.
57. SGP/Y13.
58. SGP/B/55.
59. *i.e.* 'In secret'. The practice of the Jacobite supporters to sit at a round table under a rose (The Rose of Arno, a reference to both Pretenders) moulded in the plasterwork of the ceiling. The cycle refers to the practice of everyone taking their turn in the chair, thus no one member could be classified as the leader of the club. They toasted 'the King over the Water', by passing their drinking glasses over a bowl full of water, which, like their glasses, was usually engraved with Jacobite symbols.
60. SGP/B/55.
61. SGP/B4.
62. SGP/U5.
63. SGP/Y13.
64. SGP. Green notebook, N° 6.
65. SGP/Y13.
66. Iris Woodward, *The Story of Wem*, 1952, p.40.
67. SGP/W1.

68. SGP/W9.
69. Iris Woodward, *The Story of Wem*, 1952, p.38.
70. SGP/ N14 and N18.
71. Samuel Garbet, *The History of Wem*, 1818, p.244.
72. SGP/R3. addressed to S. Garbet, OLD HALL.
73. Penoyre, John & Jane, *House in the Landscape*, 1978, p.95.
74. West, Trudy, *The Timber Framed House in England*, 1971.
75. SGP/Green notebook No.6.
76. Ibid.
77. SGP/Green notebook No.6.
78. Ibid.
79. SGP/Y13.
80. Ibid.
81. Ibid.
82. SGP/Y13.
83. Hey, D. G. *An English Rural Community, Myddle under the Tudors & Stuarts.* Leicester U.P.1974, p.86.
84. SGP/Y13.
85. SGP/C6.
86. SGP/Y13.
87. Ibid.
88. Ibid.
89. Ibid.
90. Ibid.
91. Ibid.
92. Ibid.
93. Ibid.
94. Ibid.
95. SGP/Y13.
96. Garbet, S., *The History of Wem*, 1818, p.180.
97. SGP/A12, 13, 16.
98. Mingay, G. E. *English Landed Society in the 18th Century*, 1963, p.134.
99. Mingay, G. E. *English Landed Society in the 18th Century*, 1963, p.24.
100. Mingay, G. E. *English Landed Society in the 18th Century*, 1963, p.3.
101. SGP/U5. Inventories of Samuel Garbet.
102 SGP/ Green notebook N° 6.
103. SGP/L 1–70.
104. SGP/L13.
105. SGP/L 2, 6, 59.
106. SGP/L 20.
107. SGP/L 23.
108. SGP/L 30.

109. SGP Notebook N° 4.
110. SGP/ Green notebook N° 6.
111. SGP/ Notebook N° 4.
112. SGP/ Notebook N° 4.
113. SGP/ Notebook N°ˢ 4 & 6.
114. SGP/Y13.
115. SGP/ Notebook N° 6.
116. Ibid.
117. Ibid.
118. Ibid.
119. Marshall, D. *English People in the 18th Century*, p136.
120. Mungay, G.E. *English Landed Society in the 18th Century*, 1963, p.133.
121. Briggs, A. *English Society in the 18th Century*, p.340.
122. SGP/Green notebook N° 6.
123. Wem Parish Registers, Vol IX, SRO.
124. SGP/M 10, 12, 14, 19.
125. SGP/Y13.
126 Garbet, S. *The History of Wem*, 1818, p.209.
127. SGP/Y13.
128. SGP/C11.
129. *Victoria County History, Shropshire*. Vol. 2, p.47.
130. Ibid.
131. Baily, B. *Portrait of Shropshire*, p.57.
132. Gough, R. *The History of the Parish of Myddle*. (Hoskins Edition 1968).
133. Hoskins, W.G. Introduction to *The History of Myddle*, 1968.
134. Hey, D. G. *An English Rural Community, Myddle under the Tudors & Stuarts.* Leicester U.P. 1974.
135. Hoskins, W.G. Introduction to *The History of Myddle*, 1968.
136. Wem Parish Register, Volume Vol. IX, S.R.O.
137. Wem Parish Register, Volume IX. Fly Leaf entry.
138. SRO/4351/CHA/1. Church Wardens Accounts for Wem, 1684–1734.
139 Garbet, S. *The History of Wem, 1818*. Introduction.
140. Hay, D. *An English Rural Community*, 1973, Introduction.
141. Ibid.
142. Kermode, J. *English County Histories (Lancashire)*, p.220.
143. Hindle, B. P. *Maps for Local History*, 1988, p.7.
144. S.R.O. No 3551/2.
145. S.R.O. No 3551/2.
146. SGP/Y13.
147. Ibid.
148. Ibid.
149. SGP/K20.

150. Currie & Lewis, *English County Histories*, 1994. p.20.
151. Baugh. G. C. *English County Histories (Shropshire)*, 1994, p.336.
152. Houlbrook, R. *English Family Life*, p.11.
153. Edstaston Parish Register, fly leaf, 1727.
154. Garbet, S. *The History of Wem*, 1818, p.105.
155. Garbet, S. *The History of Wem*, 1818, p.154.
156. Ibid, p.156.
157. Ibid, p.163.
158. SGP/Y13.
159. Garbet, S. *The History of Wem*, 1818, p.206.
160. Ibid, p.243.
161. Garbet, S. *The History of Wem*, 1818, p.243.
162. Ibid, p.69.
163. Ibid, p.98.
164. SGP/Y13.
165. Ibid.
166. Dr E. Ramsey, medical transcription of Samuel Garbets Records.
167. SGP/Y13. Description written by Samuel Garbet junior.

Also available from
Bridge Books:

The Dissolution of Valle Crucis Abbey
Derrick Pratt

Valle crucis Abbey, a small Cistercian monastic settlement near Llangollen, founded in the 13th century by Madog, Prince of Powys, was one of numerous religious houses destroyed during the reign of Henry VIII. Today, its ruins are a picturesque reminder of a long gone way of life. In this thoroughly researched study, the suthor examines in detail the reasons behind the closure of the Abbey and the process by which it was achieved. making use of primary sources he provides an invaluable study for anyone with an interest in 16th century political, ecclesiastical and local history.

Anglo-Welsh Wars, 1050–1300
Stuart Ivinson

Warfare along the border was endemic as the English and Welsh peoples attempted to forge themselves into nations throughout the early Mediaeval period. The culmination of this was a single English state, constantly at war with the numerous Welsh principalities until the final conquest of Wales in 1282.

Rarely was the situation a clear-cut battle between Englishmen and Welshmen. Conflicts frequently created short-term cross-border alliances. Men of both nations fought both for and against each other. Matters were further complicated by the involvement of Viking mercenaries.

This book studies the period when a united England attempted, frequently without success, to subjugate a fragmented Wales. The influence of Viking, Anglo-Saxon, Norman and Welsh tactics are all considered, as are the strategies and logistics employed for the prosecution of campaigns. They point to both how and why the war machine of the powerful Anglo-Norman state was held at bay for so long and, by way of conclusion, how the adoption of elements of each others strategies ultimately proved beneficial to both sides in the struggle.

Dr Johnson and Mrs Thrale's Tour in North Wales, 1774
Adrian Bristow

In the summer of 1774 Dr Johnson and his close friends, Mr & Mrs Thrale, travelled into north Wales. Mrs Thrale wanted to take possession of her family estate of Bachygraig, which she had recently inherited and wanted to show Johnson the splendours of north Wales. The previous year he had travelled widely in the Scottish Highlands and Western Isles with Boswell and his appetite for travel remained keen even at the age of 64. Both kept diaries of their tour, though neither was meant for publication. Mrs Thrale's is a very lively and caustic account of their journey. In this book, the diaries are accompanied by extensive notes on places, persons and houses visited and are illustrated by prints, sketch maps and photographs of their wanderings. This is the first time that these diaries have been published together in this form.

Available soon

A History of St Martins & Weston Rhyn
Neville Hurdsman

A history of these two Shropshire pariches, located on the Welsh border is scheduled for publication in late 2001. Researched and written by local historian Neville Hurdsman (author of *A History of Chirk*), this book will provide a detailed, non-academic history of the people, land, houses and industries. Fully illustrated.

The Encyclopaedia of Wrexham
W. Alister Williams

A unique publication providing data on all aspects of Wrexham's past including streets, notable buildings, people, events and organisations. Profusely illustrated. This will undoubtedly become a standard reference work on the county town of Wrexham.